1001
FUN AND FASCINATING FACTS
ABOUT TAYLOR SWIFT
YOU DIDN'T KNOW

Gwen Lively

Introduction

Welcome, Swifties!

In this book, you'll embark on an exciting journey through over 1,000 fun facts about Taylor Swift.

From her childhood and personal quirks to her incredible career achievements, this collection will explore every corner of her world.

Whether you've been a fan since the Fearless era or joined the fandom recently, this book is packed with trivia, insider details, and lesser-known facts that celebrate all things Taylor.

So, grab your favorite cardigan, get comfy, and dive into the ultimate Taylor Swift trivia experience!

Contents

1

Early Life and Childhood

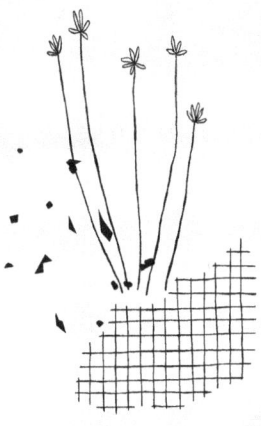

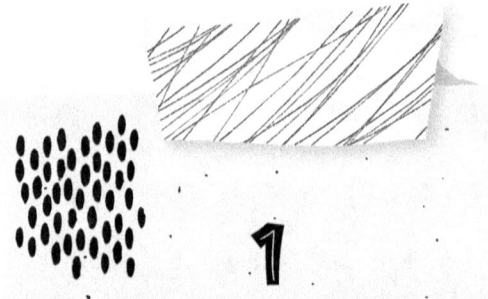

1

Taylor Swift was born on December 13, 1989, in Reading, Pennsylvania, USA.

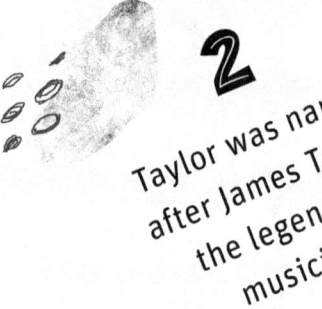

2

Taylor was named after James Taylor, the legendary musician.

3

Her childhood home was on an 11-acre Christmas tree farm in Reading, Pennsylvania.

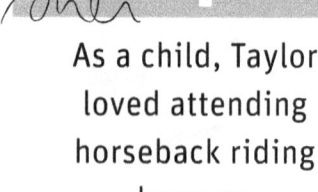

4

As a child, Taylor loved attending horseback riding lessons.

5

She first fell in love with country music after listening to Shania Twain.

7

She starred in school plays and local theater as a young girl.

6

Taylor once described her upbringing on a Christmas tree farm as "magical."

8

She was known for writing stories and poems at an early age.

9

Taylor's grandmother, Marjorie Finlay, was a professional opera singer.

11

Her younger brother, Austin, is a filmmaker and often appears in her social media posts.

10

She used to sing the national anthem at local sporting events.

12

Taylor attended Hendersonville High School but was homeschooled in her junior and senior years.

13

Taylor's father worked as a financial advisor, while her mother was a homemaker.

14

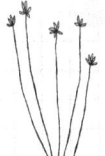

Growing up, Taylor's family attended church regularly.

15

She first learned to play guitar from a computer repairman who taught her basic chords.

16

 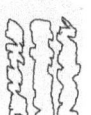

Taylor once admitted she loved watching detective shows as a kid.

17

Her love for cats began at a young age—she always wanted to adopt a pet cat.

18

Taylor was an avid reader and was particularly fond of "The Chronicles of Narnia" series.

19

As a young girl, she loved spending summers in Stone Harbor, New Jersey.

20

She wrote short stories before transitioning into songwriting.

21

Taylor was fascinated by the idea of becoming a novelist before she fell in love with music.

22

She loved decorating her notebooks and journals with glitter and stickers.

23

Taylor took voice lessons as a child to hone her singing skills.

24

She spent hours practicing guitar in her bedroom, often late into the night.

25

Her favorite subject in school was English, and she loved writing essays.

26

Her first celebrity crush was Hanson's lead singer, Zac Hanson.

27

She loved arts and crafts, particularly creating her own scrapbooks.

28

Taylor's family moved to Nashville when she was 14 to pursue her dream of becoming a country star.

29

She has said she always had a vivid imagination, which helped with her songwriting.

30

Taylor was inspired to perform after watching Faith Hill on TV.

31

She would perform at local karaoke competitions, which boosted her confidence.

32

Her first song was about a crush she had in elementary school.

33

As a child, Taylor loved making mixtapes of her favorite songs for friends.

34

She participated in many talent shows, winning several of them.

35

Taylor loved listening to her parents' old records, including classic rock and country albums.

36

She used to host mini-concerts in her family's living room for her parents and brother.

37

Taylor's favorite ice cream flavor as a kid was vanilla with rainbow sprinkles.

38

She used to write and perform plays for her family, often casting her brother as a sidekick.

39

Taylor once dressed up as a fairy for Halloween and performed songs for trick-or-treaters.

40

Her family was always supportive of her dreams, even when others doubted her.

2

Career Beginnings

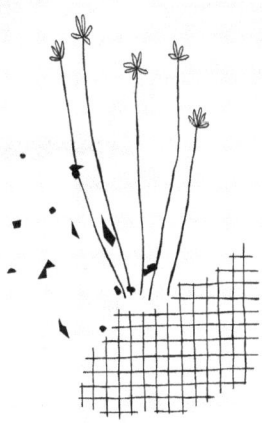

41

Taylor wrote her first album during high school while being homeschooled.

42

Her breakout single "Tim McGraw" was inspired by her first high school romance.

43

Taylor signed her first major record deal with Big Machine Records at age 14.

44

She performed at local bars and coffee shops in Nashville before getting her big break.

45

Taylor personally handed her demo CDs to record labels around Nashville.

46

Her debut album was released on October 24, 2006.

47

Taylor was the opening act for Rascal Flatts on their 2006 tour.

48

Her debut single "Tim McGraw" peaked at number 6 on the Billboard Hot Country Songs chart.

49

Taylor co-wrote every song on her debut album.

50

She was featured as the face of Abercrombie & Fitch's "Rising Stars" campaign in 2005.

51

Taylor made her first national TV appearance on Good Morning America in 2006.

52

She was the youngest person to single-handedly write and sing a number one country hit with "Our Song."

53

Taylor's first Grammy nomination came in 2008 for Best New Artist.

54

She was influenced by country legends like Loretta Lynn and Dolly Parton during her early career.

55

Taylor was heavily involved in the production and writing process for her debut album.

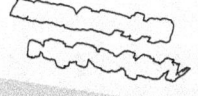

56

Her first big award win was the Horizon Award at the 2007 Country Music Association Awards.

57

Taylor used her Myspace page to connect with fans in the early days of her career.

58

She credits social media with helping her gain traction with younger fans.

59

Taylor's first big arena performance was at the Houston Rodeo in 2007.

60

She spent her teenage years balancing school with her blossoming career.

61

Taylor wrote "Teardrops on My Guitar" about a boy she had a crush on in high school.

62

She appeared as a guest performer on multiple late-night shows during her rise to fame.

63

Taylor's self-titled debut album was certified Platinum just a year after its release.

64

She often opened for larger acts like Brad Paisley and George Strait during her early years.

65

Taylor won the Songwriter/Artist of the Year Award from the Nashville Songwriters Association in 2007.

66

She was once offered a modeling contract as a teenager, but she chose music instead.

67

Taylor credits her mother with being a major influence and support throughout her early career.

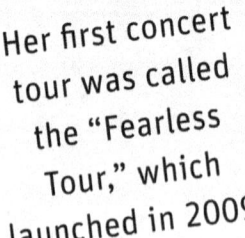

68

Her first concert tour was called the "Fearless Tour," which launched in 2009.

69

Taylor became the youngest artist in history to win Entertainer of the Year at the Academy of Country Music Awards.

70

She wrote many of her early songs on her bedroom floor using a cheap guitar.

71

Her love for storytelling started with country music and continued into her pop career.

72

Taylor had a cameo in the 2009 film Hannah Montana: The Movie.

73

She was once told she didn't have the "right look" to be a country star but proved critics wrong.

74

Taylor won the 2007 Country Music Association's Horizon Award for best new artist.

75

Her favorite performance of her debut tour was at Madison Square Garden.

76

Taylor wrote "Tied Together with a Smile" about a friend who struggled with an eating disorder.

77

She once performed at a talent show in high school, which led to local buzz about her music.

78

Taylor's early work was known for blending traditional country with modern pop influences.

79

Her first big break came when Scott Borchetta, the head of Big Machine Records, signed her in 2005.

80

Taylor has said she wrote songs to process her emotions because she felt misunderstood in school.

81

She was once compared to a young Sheryl Crow for her genre-blending sound.

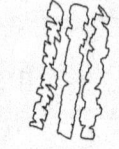

82

Taylor's breakout success came when Taylor Swift was nominated for Best New Artist at the 50th Grammy Awards.

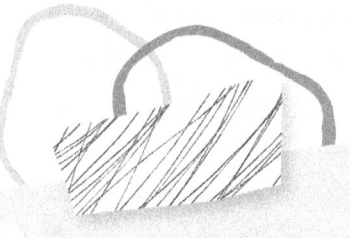

83

Her performance at the Houston Livestock Show and Rodeo drew a crowd of over 60,000 people.

84

The song "Picture to Burn" was one of the angriest breakup songs on her debut album.

85

Taylor was inspired by the Dixie Chicks and Shania Twain during her early career.

86

Her father invested in Big Machine Records, helping to kickstart her career.

87

Taylor spent many of her teenage years writing songs about unrequited love and personal heartbreaks.

88

She opened for Tim McGraw and Faith Hill on their Soul2Soul Tour.

89

Taylor wrote many of her debut album's songs about boys who didn't know she existed.

90

Her first trip to Nashville was at age 11, and it was there that she decided she wanted to become a country singer.

91

Taylor was influenced by traditional country artists like Garth Brooks and Reba McEntire during her early career.

92

Her family moved to a rented house in Hendersonville, Tennessee, to support her dream of becoming a singer.

93

Taylor appeared on The Ellen DeGeneres Show in 2006, marking one of her earliest television appearances.

94

She won a CMT Music Award for Breakthrough Video of the Year in 2007 for "Tim McGraw."

95 ★

Taylor's self-taught guitar skills helped her write her first songs and gave her a unique edge as a young artist in Nashville, where she was one of the few country singers who also played guitar at such a young age.

96

Taylor's self-titled debut album spent over 275 weeks on the Billboard 200 chart, marking one of the longest runs for an album.

97

She was featured on Rolling Stone's "New Artists to Watch" list in 2007.

98

Taylor became the first female artist to write or co-write every song on a debut platinum-certified album.

99

She was awarded the BMI Songwriter of the Year Award in 2007 at just 17 years old.

100

Taylor's appearance on The Oprah Winfrey Show in 2008 helped introduce her to a wider audience.

101

Her early single "Our Song" made Taylor the youngest person to single-handedly write and perform a number-one song on the country charts.

102

Taylor was the youngest artist ever to be nominated for CMA's Horizon Award.

103

She won her first Teen Choice Award in 2008 for Breakout Artist.

104

Her first Grammy performance was in 2008, where she sang Should've Said No.

105

Taylor was mentored by veteran country artist Tim McGraw during her early career.

106

She appeared in commercials for CoverGirl in 2009, marking her first major beauty endorsement.

107

Taylor performed at the White House in 2009 as part of a musical series organized by Michelle Obama.

108

Her song "White Horse" from the Fearless album won two Grammy Awards in 2010.

3

Musical Evolution

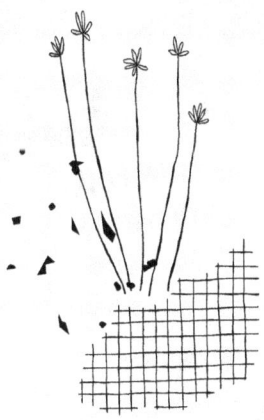

109

Taylor's Fearless album helped her go from being a country star to a bigger, mainstream artist.

110

Her 1989 album was the first time she fully switched to pop music, and she says it was one of the best choices she ever made.

111

On her Reputation album, Taylor tried new sounds like electronic and synth-pop, giving the music a darker, edgier feel.

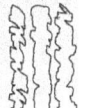

112

With Folklore and Evermore, Taylor moved into indie folk and alternative rock, which surprised her fans and music critics.

113

Taylor is known for changing her style with every new album, keeping her fans and critics excited.

114

Her song "We Are Never Ever Getting Back Together" was her first number one hit on the Billboard Hot 100 chart.

115

1989 was Taylor's first full pop album, and it won the Album of the Year Grammy.

116

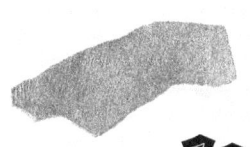

Her song "Bad Blood" had a remix featuring rapper Kendrick Lamar, which was one of her first hip-hop collaborations.

117

Taylor likes to explore different types of music in her albums, including country, pop, rock, indie, and alternative.

118

Red was loved for mixing country, rock, and pop, and it was called a genre-breaking album.

119

She says that making 1989 was her favorite album experience because it gave her more creative freedom.

120

Her Lover album had a more romantic and dreamy sound, which was different from the darker vibe of Reputation.

121

Taylor was inspired by 80s pop music while making 1989, especially by artists like Annie Lennox and Madonna.

123

Her Speak Now album was special because she wrote every song by herself, which is rare for artists.

122

Reputation was written as a response to how the media portrayed her, and it helped her take control of her story.

124

Taylor says that country music legends like Patsy Cline were big inspirations for her songwriting.

125

The re-recording of Red (Taylor's Version) broke streaming records on its release day.

126

Indie folk artists like Bon Iver inspired Taylor when she was creating Folklore and Evermore.

127

Her song "Shake It Off" from 1989 became one of the best-selling singles ever, with over 22 million copies sold.

128

She won the Grammy for Best Pop Vocal Album for 1989, showing her move from country to pop was a big success.

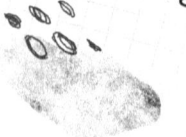

129

Taylor wrote more personal and deep lyrics in Folklore and Evermore, which she worked on during the pandemic.

130

Fearless (Taylor's Version) was the first re-recorded album to debut at number one on the Billboard 200.

131

Taylor wrote all the songs on Speak Now by herself, which is rare for an artist in the music business.

132

She says that Lana Del Rey influenced her more experimental work on Folklore.

133

The Reputation Stadium Tour became one of the highest-earning tours ever.

134

1989 was Taylor's fifth studio album, and it was loved by critics for its polished pop sound.

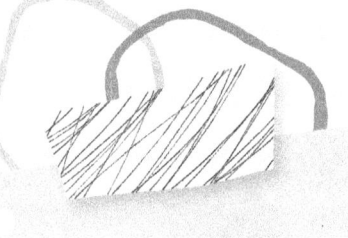

135

Taylor began trying out orchestral and indie sounds in songs like "The Last Great American Dynasty."

136

Her song "Style" from 1989 became one of the most iconic songs from her pop era.

137

Taylor says her Lover album was inspired by her desire to return to a more positive and romantic sound after Reputation.

139

The song "All Too Well" from Red is known as one of her best-written songs, with fans loving its storytelling.

138

Folklore was praised for its simple production and thoughtful lyrics, marking a new creative direction for Taylor.

140

Taylor's albums often follow a theme, with each one representing a new chapter in her life.

141

Fearless (2008) was Taylor Swift's first album to be nominated for and win Album of the Year at the Grammys.

142

Fearless was also the most-awarded country album in history at the time it came out.

143

Her song "Out of the Woods" from 1989 is remembered for her powerful vocal performance.

144

Taylor wrote all of Speak Now by herself after some people questioned her songwriting skills.

4

Iconic Awards and Achievements

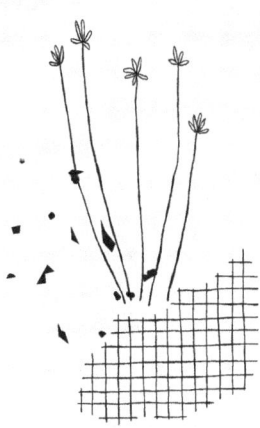

145

Taylor Swift has won more American Music Awards than anyone else, with 40 wins.

146

She became the first woman to win the Grammy Award for Album of the Year three times.

147

Taylor was the first artist to debut at number one on both the Billboard 200 and Hot 100 charts in the same week with her album Folklore and the song "Cardigan."

148

She holds the record for winning the most Billboard Music Awards for a female artist.

149

In 2019, Billboard named Taylor the Woman of the Decade for her contributions to music.

150

Taylor has won 12 Grammy Awards, making her one of the most awarded female artists ever.

151

She became the first artist to have six albums sell over 500,000 copies in just one week.

152

Taylor won the MTV Video Music Award for Best Female Video in 2009 for "You Belong with Me." This led to the famous moment when Kanye West interrupted her speech.

153

Her 1989 tour won the Top Touring Artist award at the 2016 Billboard Music Awards.

154

Taylor has been named one of Time Magazine's 100 Most Influential People in the World several times.

155

In 2016, BMI created a special Taylor Swift Award just for her, honoring her influence as a songwriter.

156

In 2009, Taylor became the youngest artist to win the CMA Entertainer of the Year award.

157

She received the Global Icon Award at the BRIT Awards, which is one of the highest honors in British music.

158

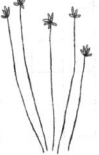

Taylor became the first artist to win the American Music Awards Artist of the Decade award in 2019.

159

She holds a Guinness World Record for the fastest-selling digital album by a female artist in 1989.

160

Taylor was the first artist ever to sell over 1 million albums in one week three different times.

161

In 2016, she won the Grammy Award for Best Music Video for "Bad Blood."

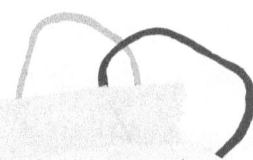

162

The Nashville Songwriters Association International (NSAI) named Taylor Songwriter of the Year seven times.

163

She is the second most-awarded female artist at the MTV Video Music Awards, with 14 wins, Beyoncé being the first.

164

Taylor's Fearless album won Album of the Year at the 2010 Grammys, making her the youngest person ever to win this award at the time.

165

Taylor won the Billboard Woman of the Year award twice, in 2011 and 2014.

166

In 2012, she became the first woman to open the iHeartRadio Music Festival.

167

Taylor set a Guinness World Record by having 10 songs simultaneously occupying the top 10 of the Billboard Hot 100.

168

Her song "Shake It Off" was nominated for three Grammy Awards, including Record of the Year.

169

Taylor was named the most charitable celebrity of 2014 by DoSomething.org because of her donations and support for different causes.

170

In 2015, she won the Brit Award for International Female Solo Artist.

171

Taylor's Reputation Stadium Tour earned over $266 million, making it the highest-earning tour in the US at that time.

172

Throughout her career, Taylor has won more than 90 major awards, including Grammys, Billboard Awards, and American Music Awards.

☆ 173

Her album Fearless (Taylor's Version) became the first re-recorded album to reach number one on the Billboard 200 chart.

175

Taylor was given an honorary doctorate of fine arts from New York University in 2022.

174

She won the Global Achievement Award at the 2020 Ivor Novello Awards for her impact on music worldwide.

☆ 176

She holds the record for the most number-one debuts on the Billboard 200 chart by a female artist.

177

Taylor was named Artist of the Year at the American Music Awards three years in a row (2018, 2019, and 2020).

179

Taylor was the first female artist to win the Brit Global Icon Award.

178

She was the first woman to win the Pinnacle Award at the CMA Awards, which honors artists who have achieved worldwide success.

180

She holds the Guinness World Record for the highest-earning tour by a solo artist.

181

Taylor was named the highest-paid celebrity in the world by Forbes magazine in 2019.

182

In 2022, she became the youngest person to receive the Songwriter/Artist of the Decade award from the Nashville Songwriters Association International (NSAI).

183

Her Lover album became the best-selling studio album worldwide in 2019.

184

Throughout her career, Taylor has broken over 58 Guinness World Records.

185

She was the first artist ever to have four albums sell over 1 million copies in their first week.

186

Billboard named her the Top Female Artist of the 2010s decade.

187

Taylor is the first artist to have both a number one album and a number one song on the Billboard charts in three different decades.

188

In 2020, Rolling Stone magazine named Taylor one of the "Greatest Artists of All Time."

189

In 2015, Taylor won the YouTube Music Award for Artist of the Year.

190

Her Red (Taylor's Version) album broke Spotify's record for the most streams in a day by a female artist.

191

Taylor has won the Best International Artist award multiple times at the ARIA Awards in Australia.

5

Personal Life and Interests

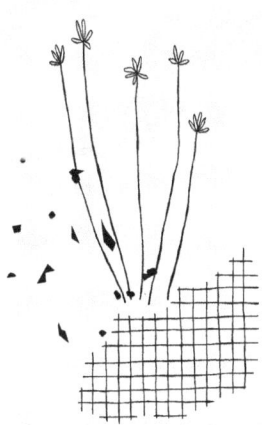

192

Taylor has three cats named Meredith Grey, Olivia Benson, and Benjamin Button, named after characters from TV and movies.

194

She loves baking and often shares pictures of her treats with her fans on social media.

193

Taylor is very private about her relationships, especially in the last few years.

195

Taylor enjoys making homemade cookies for her friends during the holidays.

196

Taylor is a huge fan of the show Grey's Anatomy and named her first cat after the lead character.

197

She describes herself as a homebody and loves staying home with her cats and close friends.

198

Taylor collects vintage typewriters and has some on display in her home.

199

Her mom, Andrea Swift, is one of Taylor's biggest supporters and has been battling cancer for several years.

200

Taylor's brother Austin works in the entertainment industry as an actor and filmmaker.

201

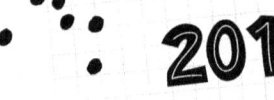

Taylor loves crime shows, especially Law & Order: SVU, which inspired her cat Olivia's name.

202

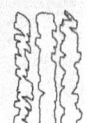

She likes sending handwritten thank-you notes to fans, friends, and people she works with.

203

Taylor often makes homemade gifts for her closest friends and family.

204

She is a big supporter of reading and enjoys sharing her favorite books with her fans.

205

Taylor loves celebrating holidays with her loved ones, and Christmas is her favorite holiday.

206

She once threw a big "Fourth of July Extravaganza" at her Rhode Island home for her friends and family.

207

Taylor loves decorating, especially for the holidays.

208

She keeps a journal where she writes down her thoughts, feelings, and ideas for songs.

209

Taylor has a sweet tooth and loves baking cakes, pies, and cookies.

210

Her favorite comfort food is chicken tenders.

211

Taylor enjoys cooking and often hosts dinner parties for her friends.

212

She owns several homes, including ones in Rhode Island, New York City, and Nashville.

213

Taylor enjoys photography and often takes pictures of her life with Polaroid cameras.

214

She likes making handmade photo albums and scrapbooks to remember special moments.

215

Taylor loves doing puzzles and often works on them in her free time.

216

She loves the ocean and often goes to her beach house in Rhode Island to relax.

217

Taylor's favorite color is blue, which reflects a more peaceful and thoughtful side of herself.

218

She has a collection of vintage vinyl records that she enjoys listening to.

219

Taylor loves Shakespeare and often uses his works as inspiration for her song lyrics.

220

She enjoys watching baking shows and says they often inspire her to bake more.

221

Taylor likes to relax by using lavender-scented candles after long days in the studio.

222

She loves floral patterns and often wears clothes with flower designs.

223

Taylor is known for hosting small dinner parties where she cooks for her guests.

224

Taylor is very interested in architecture and interior design, and she helps decorate her homes.

225

She enjoys knitting and once made a scarf for a friend as a gift.

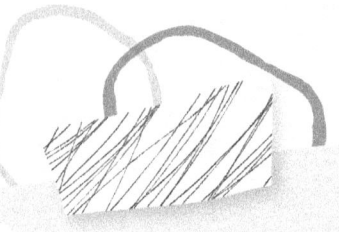

226

Taylor has said that autumn is her favorite season because she loves the cozy feeling and pretty colors.

227

She collects antique jewelry and often wears vintage-style pieces.

228

Taylor loves sending handwritten letters to her friends and people she works with.

6

Fashion and Style

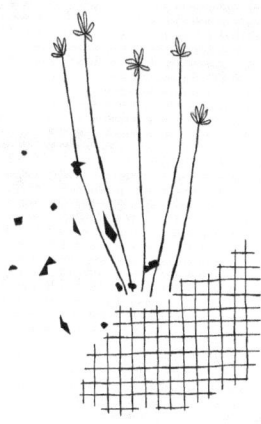

229

Taylor is famous for her red lipstick, which became a big part of her style during the Red Album era.

230

She has said that Grace Kelly and Francoise Hardy are a few of her fashion role models.

231

Taylor's style has changed over time, going from country looks to high-fashion outfits.

232

She often wore vintage-style dresses, especially during her 1989 era.

233

Taylor worked with designer Stella McCartney to create a special Lover fashion collection.

234

She has been on the covers of famous fashion magazines like Vogue, Elle, and Harper's Bazaar.

235

In her Reputation era, Taylor's style became more edgy, with leather jackets, chokers, and black boots.

236

She often wears custom-made outfits for her tours, designed by famous designers like Elie Saab and Roberto Cavalli.

237

Taylor's Folklore era featured simpler, cozy clothing with earthy colors, matching the "cottagecore" style.

238

She often wears beautiful gowns at award shows designed by famous fashion brands like Versace and Oscar de la Renta.

239

During her 1989 World Tour, Taylor wore many different costumes, including a sparkly jumpsuit and a glittery two-piece outfit.

240

In her Lover era, Taylor wore lots of pastel colors, floral patterns, and fun, romantic dresses.

241

She has walked the red carpet at the Met Gala many times, wearing stunning designer dresses.

243

She often wears high-waisted shorts and crop tops when she's out and about.

242

During her early country music days, Taylor was known for wearing sundresses and cowboy boots.

244

Taylor's love for cat-eye eyeliner became a key part of her beauty style during her pop music years.

245

She has said she feels most comfortable in a simple t-shirt and jeans when she's not performing.

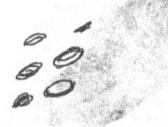

246

Taylor loves sparkles and glitter, and she often includes them in her stage outfits.

247

Her red carpet looks often have a vintage-inspired feel, giving her a classic and timeless style.

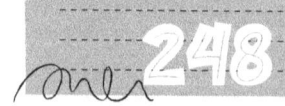

248

Taylor worked with Keds in 2012 to design her own line of sneakers.

249

She wears custom-made outfits on her tours, with detailed and unique designs.

250

At the 2016 Met Gala, Taylor's look was inspired by futuristic fashion, and she wore a silver metallic mini-dress.

251

Taylor often matches her outfits with vintage accessories like pearl earrings and classic handbags.

252

During her Red era, her fashion included bold colors, plaid patterns, and structured coats.

253

Taylor wears custom-made outfits for her album photo shoots, like the flowing gowns in her Folklore photos.

255

Taylor's Reputation Tour featured exciting stage outfits, like a bedazzled jumpsuit with a snake design.

254

She works closely with her stylists to create looks that match the themes of her albums.

256

She is known for wearing designer high heels on the red carpet, but she often switches to sneakers for comfort.

257

During her Lover era, Taylor wore bright pastel colors and romantic dresses that matched the album's themes of love and happiness.

258

Taylor loves vintage sunglasses and often wears them casually when she's out.

259

During her Speak Now era, Taylor wore fairy-tale-like gowns with flowing skirts.

260

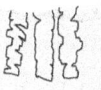

She often wears bold patterns and floral prints during the spring and summer.

261

Taylor likes to wear leather jackets and boots when she goes for a more edgy style.

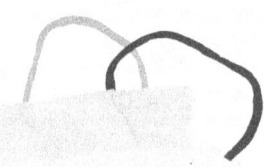

262

In her Fearless era, Taylor's style included lots of sparkles, sequins, and cowboy boots, showing her country music roots.

263

Taylor loves trying out different hairstyles, including bangs, curls, and sleek ponytails.

7

How Taylor Stays
in Shape

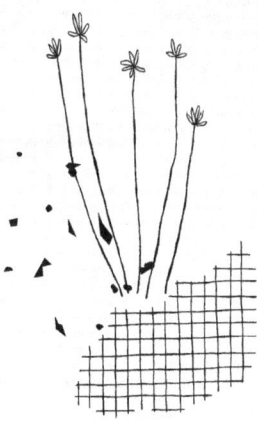

264

Taylor tries to eat healthy most of the time, but she also enjoys treats like burgers and ice cream on the weekends.

265

Taylor drinks a lot of water every day to stay hydrated.

266

She likes to dance during her concerts, which helps keep her in great shape.

267

She works with a personal trainer when she's preparing for tours to build strength and endurance.

 **268**

Taylor prefers bodyweight exercises, like squats and lunges, to help tone her muscles.

269

She enjoys hiking outdoors when she's looking for a fun way to exercise.

270

Taylor eats salads and lean proteins like chicken and fish to keep her meals healthy.

 271

She avoids sugary drinks and soda, preferring water or tea instead.

272

Taylor stretches every day to keep her muscles loose and prevent injuries.

274

Taylor sometimes works out in the morning to start her day with energy.

273

She uses light weights when she works out to build muscle without getting too bulky.

275

Taylor doesn't like strict diets, so she focuses on balance and moderation in her meals.

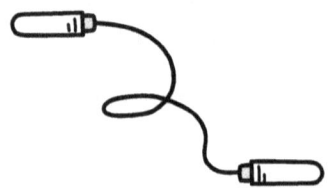

276

She listens to music while working out, which keeps her motivated and focused.

277

Taylor enjoys going for walks, especially in the city, as an easy way to stay active.

278

Taylor dances a lot while rehearsing for her tours, which is a fun way for her to stay fit.

279

She likes to eat fruit and yogurt for breakfast to give her energy for the day.

280

Taylor doesn't believe in skipping meals, so she makes sure to eat regular, healthy meals.

281

She sometimes uses a treadmill when she can't run outside, especially on tour.

282

Taylor does planks to strengthen her core and improve her overall fitness.

283

She includes lots of veggies in her meals to make sure she's getting enough nutrients.

284

Taylor loves to cook her own meals, which helps her control what she's eating.

285

She avoids fast food when she's on tour, choosing healthier options instead.

286

Taylor does resistance band exercises to tone her muscles without needing heavy equipment.

287

Taylor tries to get enough sleep every night, which is important for staying healthy and fit.

288

She takes time to
relax and unwind,
knowing that stress
can impact her health
and fitness.

8

Tour Life and Concert Magic

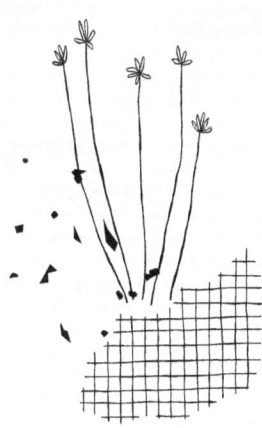

289

Taylor's Fearless Tour was her first big tour as the main artist, and it made over $63 million worldwide.

290

Her 1989 World Tour was one of the most successful tours ever, making more than $250 million.

291

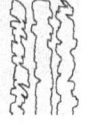

The Reputation Stadium Tour earned over $345 million, making it the highest-earning tour in U.S. history.

292

Taylor is known for inviting surprise guests, like Justin Timberlake and Mick Jagger, to perform with her during her tours.

293

Taylor's concerts are very interactive, and fans are encouraged to dress up and wear light-up bracelets.

294

Her Speak Now Tour had amazing stage designs, including a castle and a balcony that flew through the air.

295

The Red Tour featured a stage that could rotate, several costume changes, and fireworks.

296

Taylor is known for performing acoustic versions of her songs during concerts, often while on a rotating set.

297

During the Fearless Tour, Taylor wore a dress that looked like Cinderella's for her performance of "Love Story."

298

At each concert, Taylor performs a special acoustic song that's unique to that show.

299

The 1989 World Tour had a long catwalk that went into the audience so Taylor could be closer to her fans.

300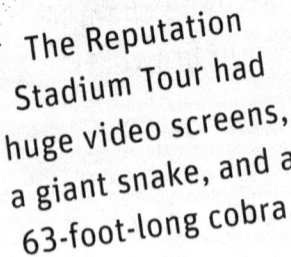

The Reputation Stadium Tour had huge video screens, a giant snake, and a 63-foot-long cobra.

301

Taylor loves surprising her fans by performing rare songs or ones that haven't been released yet.

303

On the Red Tour, Taylor used a big floating platform that let her sing above the crowd.

302

She is known for making dramatic entrances at her concerts, like rising up from under the stage or flying over the audience.

304

She changes the setlist for each city she performs in, making every concert special for the fans.

305

During the Fearless Tour, there was a cool "rain shower" effect while she performed "Should've Said No."

9

Special Fan Moments

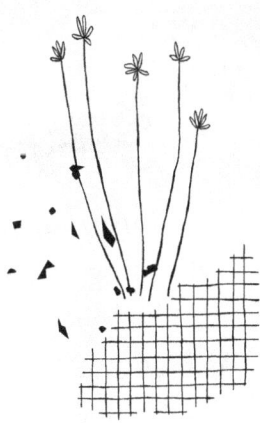

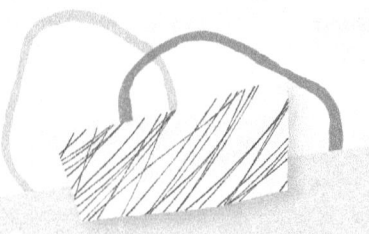

306

Taylor often hosts "Secret Sessions," where she invites fans to her home to listen to her albums before they are released.

308

Once, Taylor sent a fan $1,989 to help her pay her student loans after hearing about her financial struggles.

307

She likes to interact with fans on social media, often liking their posts and leaving comments.

309

Taylor is known for hiding "Easter eggs" in her music videos and social media posts for fans to figure out.

310

Her song "You Belong With Me" became a favorite among high school students and was featured in many school performances.

312

Taylor has a Tumblr account where she talks to fans and responds to their posts.

311

She once invited a fan to her house for cookies after seeing the fan had traveled from another country to attend her concert.

313

Taylor is known for sending personalized gifts to fans during the holiday season, something she calls "Swiftmas."

314

She once donated $50,000 to a fan's GoFundMe page after learning that the fan's family was struggling with medical bills.

315

Her "Bad Blood" music video featured many of her famous friends, like Gigi Hadid, Selena Gomez, and Karlie Kloss.

316

Taylor is known for keeping her album releases secret and dropping clues on social media for fans to figure out.

317

Her influence goes beyond music, as her outfits, hairstyles, and lyrics often start trends in pop culture.

318

Once, she surprised a young fan battling cancer with a private meet-and-greet before her concert.

319

Taylor was featured in the popular video game Band Hero, where fans could play as her character.

320

Taylor once surprised a fan at their wedding and performed her song "Shake It Off."

321

Her documentary Miss Americana gave fans a behind-the-scenes look at her life, career, and personal struggles.

322

Taylor's fanbase, known as the "Swifties," is one of the most loyal and dedicated fan groups in music history.

323

She often surprises fans by helping pay off their medical bills or giving them financial support when they are struggling.

324

Taylor's surprise appearance at a fan's wedding became a viral moment in the early 2010s.

325

She likes to comment on and like her fans' TikToks, which has created many fun viral moments.

326

She dedicated her performance of "The Best Day" to a fan who lost their mother, bringing the audience to tears.

327

She once attended a fan's bridal shower in Ohio, giving them handmade gifts and personalized letters.

328

Taylor is known for replying to fans' direct messages on Instagram, often surprising them with her responses.

329

Taylor's Lover mural in Nashville became a popular tourist spot where fans gathered to celebrate her music.

330

She has sent personalized notes and flowers to fans who celebrated their birthdays with Taylor-themed parties.

332

Taylor often surprises her fans with new merchandise and exclusive items.

331

Her Folklore and Evermore albums became huge hits overnight, with fans trying to figure out hidden meanings in the lyrics for months.

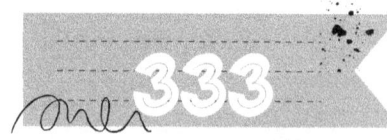

333

She frequently visits fans in hospitals and children's wards, giving them personal gifts and spending time with them.

334

She once sent a fan a handmade Christmas wreath as part of her "Swiftmas" tradition.

336

During the 1989 World Tour, Taylor invited fans backstage after every show for personal meet-and-greets.

335

Taylor is known for signing her fans' copies of her albums during random public appearances, like at Starbucks or in airports.

337

She often gives special shoutouts to her most dedicated fans during her live shows, creating memorable moments for them.

10

Taylor in Pop Culture

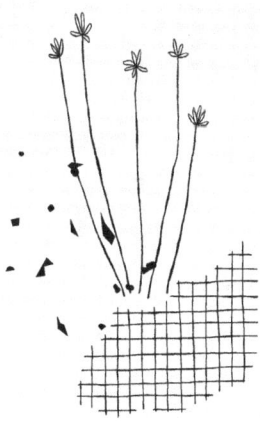

338

Taylor made a small appearance in the 2010 romantic comedy Valentine's Day, where she played a cheerful high school student.

339

Her song "Today Was a Fairytale" was featured in the soundtrack for the movie Valentine's Day.

340

In 2012, Taylor voiced the character Audrey in the animated movie The Lorax.

341

She has been a musical guest on Saturday Night Live multiple times, including a memorable performance of her song "Back to December."

342

Taylor's relationship with Joe Jonas and their breakup inspired her song "Forever & Always" on her Fearless album.

344

Taylor's close friendships with other celebrities like Gigi Hadid, Blake Lively, and Selena Gomez are often called her "Squad."

343

Her public feud with Kanye West and Kim Kardashian became one of the biggest pop culture moments of the 2010s.

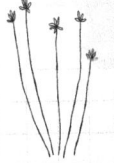

345

She made a guest appearance on the TV show New Girl in 2013, playing the role of Elaine, a wedding guest.

346

Taylor's "Bad Blood" music video won the MTV VMA for Best Music Video in 2015 and became a huge cultural moment.

347

She once surprised fans by releasing her new single, "Look What You Made Me Do," during the 2017 MTV VMAs.

11

Philanthropy and Activism

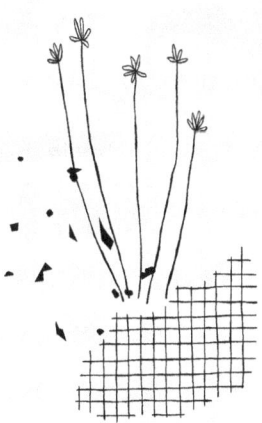

348

Taylor donated $100,000 to help rebuild a local Nashville landmark after it was damaged by flooding.

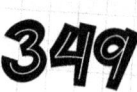

349

Taylor donated $1 million to help people affected by the 2016 Louisiana floods.

350

She cares a lot about music education and has donated millions to schools and music programs all over the U.S.

351

Taylor once donated $250,000 to help singer Kesha with legal fees during her lawsuit against Dr. Luke.

☆ 352

She often gives money from her concerts to different charities, including those helping with disaster relief and education.

353

Taylor once gave $10,000 to a fan battling cancer after finding out they had traveled to her concert.

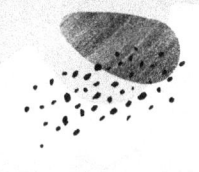

354

She donated $50,000 to the Seattle Symphony to to recognize the Symphony's contemporary classical performances.

☆ 355

Taylor has supported many organizations like the Red Cross, UNICEF, and Stand Up to Cancer.

356

During the holiday season, she frequently donates to food banks and shelters.

357

In 2020, Taylor donated $1 million to help tornado victims through the Tennessee Emergency Response Fund.

358

She speaks out for women's rights and gender equality, supporting the #MeToo movement.

359

Taylor has been helping local Nashville charities for over 10 years, including donating books to public libraries.

360

She gave to the Malala Fund, a charity that works to help girls around the world get an education.

361

In 2020, she donated $300,000 to help with tornado relief in Nashville and encouraged her fans to help too.

362

Taylor has quietly donated to fans in need, including helping families during the COVID-19 pandemic.

363

Taylor gave $500,000 to help with flood relief efforts in Nashville in 2010.

364

She has supported MusiCares, a charity that helps musicians with medical and financial needs.

365

Taylor often encourages her fans to register to vote, especially during important U.S. elections.

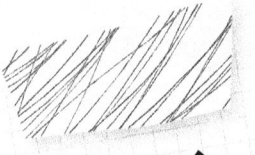

366

She worked with Feeding America to donate money and food during the COVID-19 pandemic.

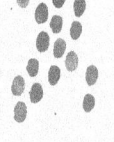

367

Throughout her career, she has donated over $1 million to different disaster relief funds.

368

Taylor's charitable work earned her the Ripple of Hope Award from the Robert F. Kennedy Human Rights organization in 2012.

369

She gave money from her 1989 World Tour to help create music scholarships at several colleges.

370

She has donated a lot to programs that help young people learn to read and write across the U.S.

12

Taylor's Love for Writing and Poetry

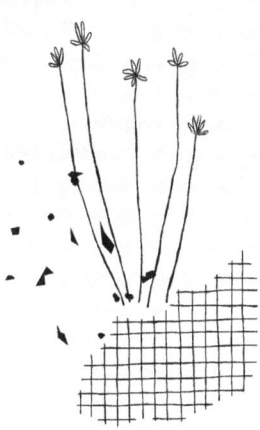

371

Taylor has been writing poetry since she was a young girl, and many of her early poems later became songs.

372

She published a poem called "Why She Disappeared" in the booklet of her Reputation album.

373

People often compare Taylor's songwriting to poetry because of the vivid pictures she paints and the stories she tells.

374

Her song "The Lakes" from Folklore talks about her love for poetry and finding a quiet place to be creative.

375

She often uses metaphors and literary references in her lyrics, drawing comparisons to famous poets like Emily Dickinson and Robert Frost.

376

Taylor has said that writing helps her work through her emotions, and she uses journaling as a type of therapy.

377

Her songwriting is known for its attention to detail, with many lyrics featuring clever wordplay and hidden meanings.

378

Taylor once shared that she keeps a notebook full of ideas, phrases, and possible song lyrics that she uses when writing new music.

379

She is influenced by famous books and has referenced stories like The Great Gatsby and Pride and Prejudice in her songs.

380

Taylor's love for poetry can be seen in her Evermore album, where she used more abstract, poetic storytelling.

381

She has said that one of her favorite authors is F. Scott Fitzgerald, and his books have inspired her songwriting.

382

Taylor's lyrics are often praised for blending deep emotions with poetic style.

383

Her song "All Too Well" is considered one of her greatest lyrical works, with fans closely analyzing every line for its deeper meaning.

384

She enjoys writing letters to her friends and fans, thinking it's a more personal way to communicate.

385

Taylor has mentioned that she writes poetry not just for her music but also as a way to capture her thoughts and feelings.

386

Her song "Seven" from Folklore is seen as a poetic, nostalgic look at childhood friendships.

387

Taylor often writes songs from different perspectives, similar to how a novelist writes from the point of view of different characters.

388

he has said that she finds inspiration for her songwriting in classic books, movies, and her own life experiences.

13

Record-Breaking Moments

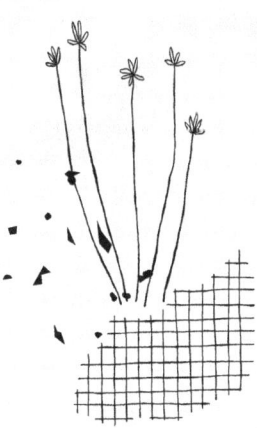

389

Taylor became the first woman to win the Grammy Award for Album of the Year three times for Fearless, 1989, and Folklore.

390

She is the only artist to debut at number one on both the Billboard 200 and Hot 100 in the same week with Folklore and the song "Cardigan."

391

Taylor's 1989 album became the first album to sell over 1 million copies in its first week.

392

Her Reputation Stadium Tour became the highest-grossing U.S. tour of all time, making over $345 million.

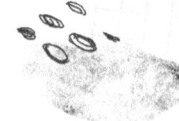

393

Taylor was the youngest artist to win the CMA's Entertainer of the Year Award in 2009.

394

She holds the Guinness World Record for the fastest-selling digital album by a female artist for 1989.

395

She has had eight albums debut at number one on the Billboard 200.

396

Taylor's Fearless album became the most awarded country album in history.

397

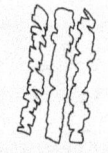

She was the first woman to debut at number one on the Billboard Hot 100 with a solo-written song, "We Are Never Ever Getting Back Together."

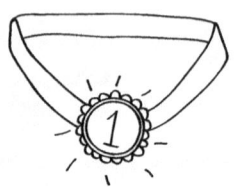

398

Taylor was the first artist to win Billboard's Woman of the Year Award twice, in 2011 and 2014.

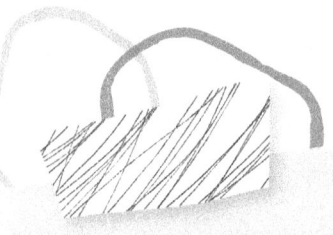

399

Her Folklore album was the first album in 2020 to spend its first six weeks at number one on the Billboard 200.

400

Taylor's Red (Taylor's Version) set a Spotify record for the most streams in a single day by a female artist.

401

She was the first artist in history to sell over 1 million albums in a week four times with Speak Now, Red, 1989 and Fearless.

402

Taylor's 1989 became the best-selling album of 2014, and she was the top-selling artist that year.

403

In 2022, Taylor became the first U.S. artist to win the Brit Global Icon Award.

404

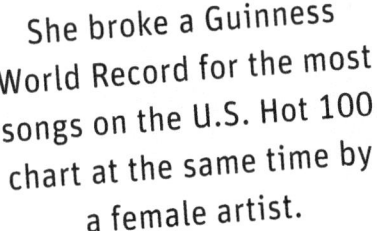

She broke a Guinness World Record for the most songs on the U.S. Hot 100 chart at the same time by a female artist.

405

Taylor was the youngest person ever to write and sing a number-one country hit with her song "Our Song."

406

She was the first artist to have four albums sell more than 1 million copies in their first week.

407

Her Speak Now album was the first to have songs completely written by Taylor with no co-writers, which is rare in the music industry.

14

Taylor's Impact on the Music Industry

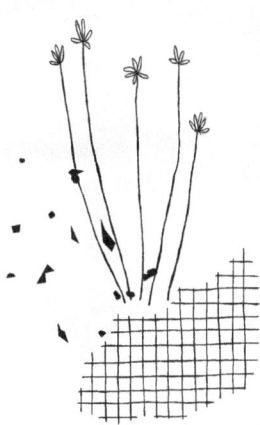

408

Taylor played a big part in getting Apple Music to pay artists during their free trial period, which led to a major change in the music industry.

409

Her decision to re-record her albums after losing ownership of her original recordings is seen as a huge moment in the fight for artist rights.

410

She has been a leader in mixing country and pop music, helping to connect Nashville with mainstream pop music.

411

Taylor's open letter to Apple in 2015 made the company change its policy and start paying artists fairly for streaming.

412

She has spoken out for songwriters, pointing out unfair practices in the music industry.

414

In 2014, she took her music off Spotify, which started a global conversation about how artists get paid for streaming.

413

Taylor was one of the first artists to use social media a lot to build a personal connection with her fans.

415

By re-recording her albums (called Taylor's Version), she set a new example for artists to take back control of their original recordings.

416

Taylor is credited with bringing country music to a younger and more mainstream audience with her early albums.

418

Taylor has used her platform to bring attention to the issue of artist ownership, helping make the music industry more open about it.

417

Her talent for mixing different types of music has inspired a generation of artists to try new styles and sounds.

419

She was one of the first artists to use Tumblr to connect with fans, inspiring other musicians to do the same.

420

Taylor's use of hidden messages and Easter eggs in her music has set a new standard for how artists engage with their fans.

421

Her fight to get fair pay from streaming services helped start a bigger conversation about how valuable music is in the digital world.

422

Taylor has been recognized for empowering female artists in an industry that is mostly run by men.

423

Her success has inspired many young women to follow their dreams in music, songwriting, and performing.

424

Taylor's ability to move between country, pop, and indie music has set a new example for artists to reinvent themselves.

425

Her personal songwriting, based on her own life, has influenced many artists to write more honestly about their feelings.

426

Taylor has played a big role in bringing back vinyl records, with many of her albums released as special-edition vinyls.

15

Iconic
Performances

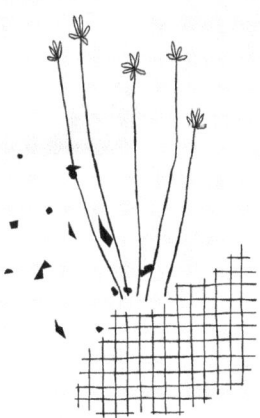

427

Taylor performed "Fifteen" with Miley Cyrus at the 2009 Grammy Awards.

428

At the 2013 Victoria's Secret Fashion Show, she performed her hit song "I Knew You Were Trouble," creating a memorable pop culture moment.

428

Her 2014 MTV VMA performance of "Shake It Off" showed her complete move to pop music.

430

Taylor headlined the 2015 Brit Awards with an amazing performance of "Blank Space."

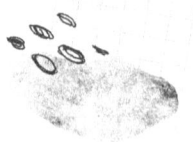

431

At the 2009 MTV Video Music Awards, Taylor's acceptance speech was interrupted by Kanye West, creating one of the most famous moments in VMA history.

432

She opened the 2012 Grammy Awards with a circus-themed performance of "We Are Never Ever Getting Back Together."

433

In 2021, Taylor performed "All Too Well (10-Minute Version)" on Saturday Night Live, and it became one of the most talked-about performances of the year.

434

Her 2018 performance at the American Music Awards had a snake-themed stage for her song "I Did Something Bad."

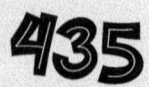

435

At the 2010 Grammy Awards, Taylor performed a mix of "Today Was a Fairytale" and "You Belong with Me."

436

Taylor performed an emotional version of "Soon You'll Get Better" during the Global Citizen One World: Together at Home concert in 2020.

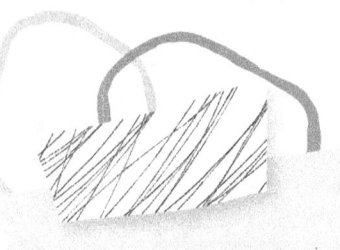

437

At the 2022 MTV VMAs, she surprised everyone with a medley of her biggest hits and revealed a new single.

438

Taylor's Reputation Stadium Tour concert film, released on Netflix, became a fan favorite and captured one of her most successful tours.

439

She performed "Lover" live at the 2019 MTV VMAs, bringing a romantic and colorful performance to the stage.

440

Taylor's acoustic performance of "Mean" at the 2011 Grammy Awards earned her a standing ovation.

441

At the 2016 Grammy Awards, she gave a powerful performance of "Out of the Woods."

442

In 2019, Taylor performed a medley of her biggest hits at the American Music Awards to celebrate winning Artist of the Decade.

443

She delivered an emotional and raw performance of "All Too Well" during her Red Tour.

444

Her performance of "You Belong With Me" at the 2009 CMA Awards is remembered as one of her best live country performances.

16

Taylor's Business Ventures and Entrepreneurship

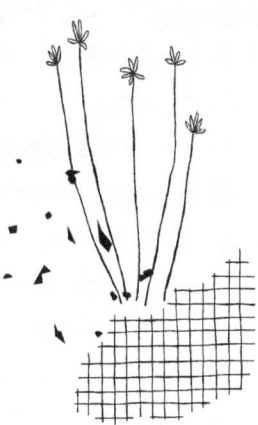

445

Taylor has launched several successful merchandise lines, including special clothing, jewelry, and accessories tied to her album releases.

446

She was one of the first artists to work with Keds, creating a line of sneakers inspired by her personal style.

447

In 2013, Taylor partnered with Diet Coke, which helped her expand her brand into the beverage world.

448

She worked with Apple Music to create exclusive behind-the-scenes content, showing fans how she makes her music.

449

Taylor's partnership with Target has led to special deluxe editions of her albums being sold only through that store.

450

She has appeared in many commercials for brands like CoverGirl, AT&T, and Capital One.

451

Taylor owns several expensive homes in New York, Los Angeles, and Nashville.

452

She co-wrote and helped produce the documentary Miss Americana, which gave fans a look into her life and career.

453

She was the first artist to sell an album with a special bundle that included concert tickets, starting a new trend in the music industry.

454

Taylor launched her own mobile app called The Swift Life, which let fans connect with her and with each other.

455

Taylor is known for buying and selling luxury real estate, making large profits from her property investments.

456

Taylor's decision to re-record her albums has set a new example for how artists can control their own music.

457

She negotiated a huge deal with Universal Music Group to make sure that she would own her future music recordings.

458

Taylor has used her merchandise and tours to create a special experience for fans, including limited-edition items and personalized gifts.

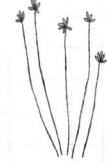

459

She created a line of Taylor Swift-themed greeting cards and gift items for American Greetings.

460

Her work in getting control of her master recordings and re-recording rights is seen as a groundbreaking move for artists' business rights.

17

Taylor's Influence on Fashion

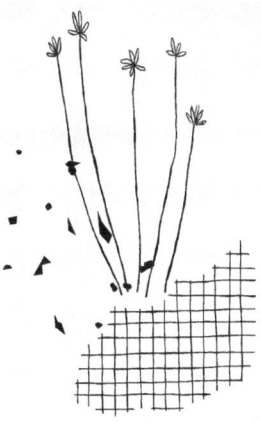

461

When she changed from a country singer to a pop star, her fashion also changed. She started wearing tailored suits, crop tops, and bold accessories.

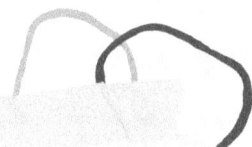

462

During her Red era, Taylor's signature look included red lipstick, high-waisted shorts, and vintage-style dresses.

463

She has walked the red carpet at the Met Gala many times, each time wearing a new fashion style to match the theme.

464

In 2011, Taylor became the face of CoverGirl, promoting their new makeup line.

465

Her outfits for the 1989 World Tour were made by top fashion designers like Roberto Cavalli.

466

Taylor worked with designer Stella McCartney to create a special Lover fashion line, which had colorful and fun designs.

467

Her everyday style, called "street style," is often praised for mixing fancy designer clothes with more affordable brands.

468

During her Reputation era, Taylor changed her style to be darker and more edgy, wearing leather jackets, combat boots, and smoky makeup.

469

In her Speak Now and Fearless eras, Taylor's love for vintage-inspired sundresses became a big trend for her fans.

18

Taylor's Homes and Real Estate

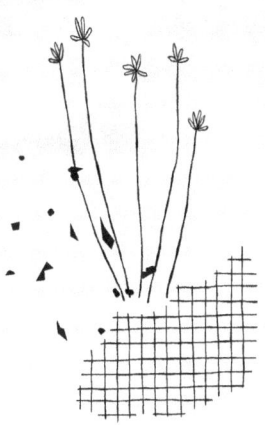

470

Taylor owns a large penthouse in Tribeca, New York City, where she often hangs out with her famous friends, hosting movie nights and holiday parties.

471

Taylor's mansion in Rhode Island, called "Holiday House," was bought for $17.75 million in 2013 and is located in Watch Hill.

472

This Rhode Island home inspired her song "The Last Great American Dynasty" from her Folklore album.

473

She also owns a historic four-story townhouse in New York City that has its own home theater and gym.

474

In 2015, she purchased a $25 million mansion in Beverly Hills, which used to belong to Hollywood legend Samuel Goldwyn.

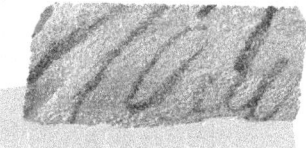

475

Taylor sold her Beverly Hills home in 2020 after restoring it and getting it declared a historic landmark.

476

She has a large estate in Nashville, where she has written and recorded many of her albums.

477

While working on her Reputation album, she rented a luxurious mansion in London.

478

Her Rhode Island mansion is famous for hosting her Fourth of July parties, with celebrity guests like Blake Lively, Ryan Reynolds, and Gigi Hadid.

479

Her Nashville home has a koi pond, and Taylor has said she enjoys spending quiet mornings by the water while writing songs.

480

Her New York townhouse is connected to her other Tribeca properties, giving her a private place to escape in the busy city.

481

Taylor also owns a private jet, which she uses to travel between her homes and to tour locations.

482

Her Rhode Island mansion sits on five acres of land and has beautiful views of the Atlantic Ocean.

483

Taylor's Nashville estate is known for its Southern charm, with a wrap-around porch and a swimming pool.

484

She often renovates and updates her homes to match her changing tastes and needs.

485

Taylor loves interior design and has been personally involved in decorating many of her homes.

486

Many of her homes have art pieces that show her love for music and literature, like vintage typewriters and framed song lyrics.

19

Iconic
Music Videos

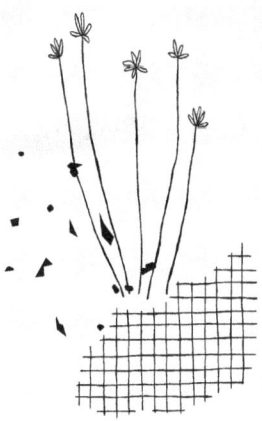

487

Taylor's "You Belong with Me" music video became one of her early hits and was nominated for Video of the Year at the MTV VMAs in 2009.

488

Her "Love Story" music video had a storyline inspired by Romeo and Juliet, with old-fashioned costumes and a castle setting.

489

The music video for "Blank Space" was filmed at the historic Oheka Castle in New York and became a huge cultural moment.

490

"Bad Blood" was nominated at the Grammy Award for Best Music Video and featured a star-studded cast, including Selena Gomez, Cara Delevingne, and Karlie Kloss.

491

Taylor's "Look What You Made Me Do" music video broke records by getting over 43 million views on YouTube in just 24 hours.

492

Her "Shake It Off" video showed fun dance routines, including ballerinas, cheerleaders, and hip-hop dancers, highlighting her playful side.

493

The "Style" music video is known for its dreamy visuals that match the song's cool vibe.

494

Taylor's "Cardigan" music video from Folklore introduced her cottagecore style, with magical forest scenes and themes of nostalgia and lost love.

495

In "The Man" music video, Taylor turns into a male version of herself to point out gender inequality and unfair treatment in the entertainment industry.

496

The "ME!" music video, featuring Brendon Urie, was a colorful celebration of being yourself, with rainbows, butterflies, and fun backdrops.

497

Taylor's "We Are Never Ever Getting Back Together" video included fun costume changes, with her wearing everything from pajamas to a 1950s-style dress.

498

Her "Out of the Woods" video was filmed in New Zealand and showed beautiful natural scenery, like snowy mountains and crashing waves.

499

The "Delicate" video shows Taylor dancing through different public places, showing off a more playful and carefree side of her.

500

The "All Too Well (10-Minute Version)" short film, directed by Taylor, starred Sadie Sink and Dylan O'Brien and was praised for its emotional storytelling.

501

The "I Knew You Were Trouble" video was one of Taylor's first steps into a more edgy pop-punk style, with dramatic visuals and a strong storyline.

502

Her "Mean" music video had a message about anti-bullying and a story about overcoming tough challenges.

503

The "Mine" video was filmed in Portland, Maine, and followed a love story that lasts for decades, showing a young couple growing together.

504

In the "Lover" music video, each room of the house represents a different part of Taylor's career, with colors and styles showing her different albums.

20

Awards and Recognitions

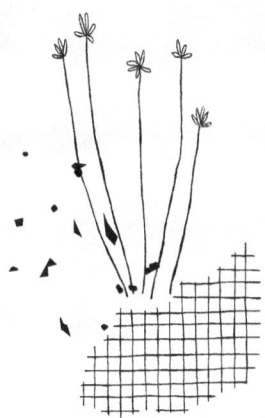

505

Taylor has won 12 Grammy Awards, making her one of the most awarded female artists in Grammy history.

506

She has been nominated for over 40 Grammy Awards during her career.

507

Taylor is the most awarded artist in the history of the American Music Awards (AMAs), with 34 wins.

508

In 2019, she was given the Artist of the Decade award at the AMAs for her impact on the music industry.

509

Taylor has won 29 Billboard Music Awards, including the Top Artist award multiple times.

511

In 2022, Taylor was named Songwriter/Artist of the Decade by the Nashville Songwriters Association International.

510

She received the Global Icon Award at the 2021 Brit Awards, becoming the first woman to win it.

512

She was the youngest person to ever receive the Pinnacle Award at the CMA Awards.

513

Taylor was honored with the Michael Jackson Video Vanguard Award at the 2015 MTV VMAs for her contributions to music videos.

515

Taylor received the Hal David Starlight Award from the Songwriters Hall of Fame for her songwriting achievements.

514

She has won several iHeartRadio Music Awards, including Female Artist of the Year.

516

She was given the Billboard Woman of the Decade Award for her influence on the music industry in the 2010s.

517

Taylor won the Brit Award for International Female Solo Artist in 2015.

518

She has been named one of Time magazine's 100 Most Influential People in the World several times.

519

Taylor was included on Forbes' list of the World's 100 Most Powerful Women for her business skills and influence.

520

She holds the Guinness World Record for the most-streamed album in a single day by a female artist for Red (Taylor's Version).

521

Taylor received the Dick Clark Award for Excellence at the American Music Awards in 2014.

522

She was given the Ultimate Choice Award at the Teen Choice Awards, which is the show's highest honor.

523

In 2021, Taylor received the Icon Award at the iHeartRadio Music Awards for her contributions to music and culture.

524

She is the only female artist to have five albums sell over one million copies in their first week.

21

Taylor's Collaborations with Other Artists

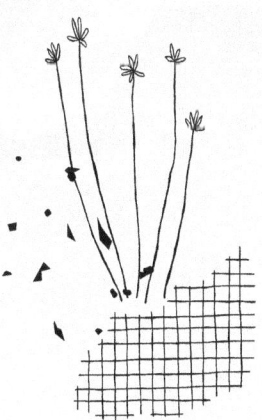

525

Taylor performed a live duet with T-Pain in 2009, doing a playful parody called "Thug Story."

526

She worked with John Mayer on the song "Half of My Heart" in 2009, and they performed it together live.

527

Taylor's collaboration with The Civil Wars on the song "Safe & Sound" for The Hunger Games soundtrack in 2012 marked a darker, haunting sound.

528

She worked with Ed Sheeran on "Everything Has Changed" from her Red album in 2012, her first major pop duet.

529

She teamed up with country star Tim McGraw for the song "Highway Don't Care" in 2013, a nod to her country roots.

530

Taylor co-wrote "Better Man" for the country group Little Big Town in 2016, and it later won a CMA Award for Song of the Year.

531

Her song "This Is What You Came For," co-written with Calvin Harris, was released in 2016 and became a hit for Calvin and Rihanna.

532

She collaborated with Kendrick Lamar for a remix of her hit song "Bad Blood" in 2015, adding a hip-hop edge to the track.

533

During her 1989 World Tour in 2015, Taylor invited her friend Selena Gomez to perform on stage, highlighting their close friendship.

534

She teamed up with Zayn Malik for the song "I Don't Wanna Live Forever" on the Fifty Shades Darker soundtrack in 2016.

535

In 2017, she released "End Game," a pop and rap collaboration featuring Ed Sheeran and Future on her Reputation album.

536

Taylor co-wrote the song "Babe" for the band Sugarland in 2018, which became a hit in the country genre.

537

Her duet with Brendon Urie from Panic! At The Disco, "ME!," was released as the lead single for her Lover album in 2019.

538

In 2019, she collaborated with Shawn Mendes for a remix of her song "Lover."

539

She featured The Chicks on her song "Soon You'll Get Better" from Lover in 2019, a deeply emotional song about her mother's cancer battle.

540

Taylor worked with Bon Iver on "Exile" from her Folklore album in 2020, marking a shift to indie folk music.

541

She collaborated closely with Aaron Dessner from The National for her Folklore and Evermore albums in 2020, giving her music an indie influence.

542

Taylor teamed up with HAIM on the song "No Body, No Crime" from Evermore in 2020, a crime-inspired track.

543

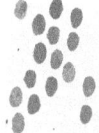

Throughout her career, Taylor has had Keith Urban as a surprise guest on stage during her Speak Now and Red tours, honoring her country roots.

544

Taylor has expressed admiration for Paul McCartney and Bruce Springsteen, mentioning that they would be dream collaborations for her one day.

22

Taylor's Close Friendships and Squad

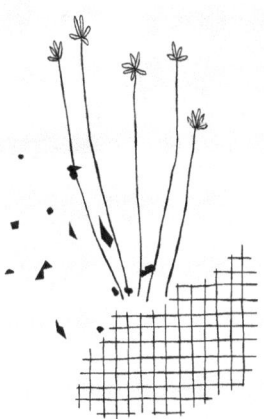

545

Taylor's friendship with Selena Gomez is one of the most famous in pop culture, and they have supported each other through big life events.

546

She became good friends with Blake Lively and Ryan Reynolds after meeting through mutual friends, and she often spends time with their family.

547

Taylor's friendship with Karlie Kloss was a big part of her "squad," and they even appeared together on the cover of Vogue.

548

She has a close bond with Gigi Hadid, who often attends Taylor's album release parties and shows.

549

Taylor's squad appeared in her "Bad Blood" music video, with famous cameos from Cara Delevingne, Hailee Steinfeld, and Zendaya.

551

Taylor and Emma Stone have been friends for over a decade, supporting each other's acting and music careers.

550

She has been close friends with Ed Sheeran for many years, and he has called her one of his biggest musical inspirations.

552

Taylor and Lorde have a close friendship, and they often spend time together in New York City when Lorde visits from New Zealand.

553

She stays in touch with many of her famous friends by sending handwritten notes, flowers, or gifts for special occasions.

554

Taylor's childhood best friend, Abigail Anderson, inspired the song "Fifteen," and they are still close today.

555

She has been friends with Jaime King for years, and Taylor is the godmother to Jaime's son, Leo.

556

Taylor is close friends with Blake Lively, and Blake's children were mentioned in Taylor's song "Betty" from her Folklore album.

557

Her group of friends, called her "squad," became a big part of pop culture in the mid-2010s, and Taylor hosted many high-profile events for them.

558

She threw a famous Fourth of July party in 2016, with her squad attending, including Ruby Rose, Cara Delevingne, and Martha Hunt.

559

She has been friends with musician Jack Antonoff for a long time, and he has co-written and produced many of her songs, including tracks on 1989, Reputation, and Folklore.

560

Taylor's friendship with model Lily Aldridge led to them working together on fashion and music projects over the years.

23

Memorable Tour Moments

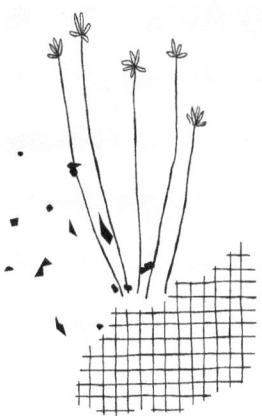

561

Taylor's 1989 World Tour had surprise guest appearances at almost every show, including Justin Timberlake, Alanis Morissette, and The Weeknd.

562

Her Fearless Tour was the first time she headlined big arenas, which was a big moment in her career.

563

During her Speak Now World Tour, Taylor performed a special acoustic set in every city, where she would cover a song by a local artist.

564

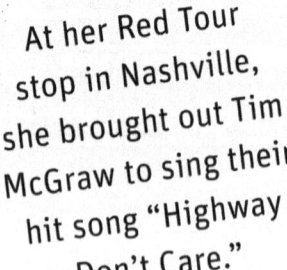

At her Red Tour stop in Nashville, she brought out Tim McGraw to sing their hit song "Highway Don't Care."

565

During the Reputation Stadium Tour, Taylor performed an emotional acoustic version of "All Too Well," leaving fans touched.

567

She performed an acoustic version of "Holy Ground" during the Red Tour, which became a fan favorite.

566

Taylor's Fearless Tour featured a special rain shower effect during her performance of "Should've Said No," creating a memorable moment.

568

During her 1989 World Tour, Taylor surprised fans by singing a duet with Mick Jagger, performing "(I Can't Get No) Satisfaction."

569

At the Reputation Stadium Tour, she surprised fans by performing "Our Song," a throwback to her early country music days.

570

Taylor's 1989 tour stop in Los Angeles featured a surprise appearance by Ellen DeGeneres, who joined her on stage in a sparkly outfit.

571

She brought out Selena Gomez during the 1989 World Tour to perform "Good for You," which was one of the first times they performed together.

572

During the Reputation Stadium Tour, Taylor sang "The Lucky One" as a special tribute to her early success and the pressures of fame.

573

Taylor's Lover Fest was planned to be her biggest tour yet, but it was canceled due to the COVID-19 pandemic.

574

She surprised the crowd during the 1989 World Tour by bringing out John Legend to perform his hit song "All of Me."

575

During her Reputation Stadium Tour, Taylor closed each show with a fireworks display while performing "This Is Why We Can't Have Nice Things."

24

Taylor's Impact on Pop Culture

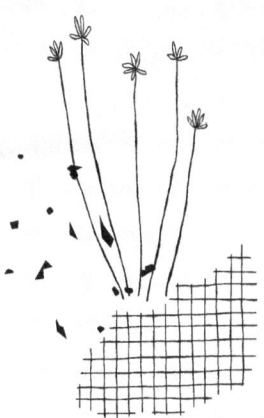

576

Taylor's song "Shake It Off" became a viral hit, inspiring many dance challenges and covers on YouTube and TikTok.

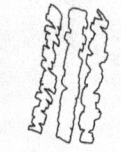

577

Her "Bad Blood" music video became a big deal, with celebrity cameos and starting conversations about female empowerment.

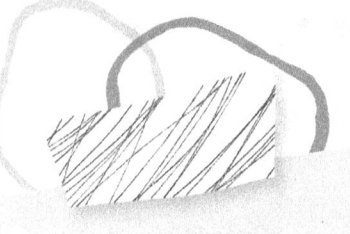

578

Taylor's switch from country music to pop with her 1989 album changed the genre and influenced many artists to try pop crossover music.

579

Her public feud with Kanye West, which started at the 2009 MTV VMAs, became one of the most talked-about events in pop culture history.

580

Taylor's decision to re-record her albums set a new example for artists to take back control of their original music recordings.

581

She made the "squad" trend popular in the mid-2010s, with her famous friends becoming a major part of pop culture.

582

Taylor's fashion journey, from cowboy boots and sundresses to high fashion and street style, has been featured in many fashion magazines.

583

Her bold move to remove her music from Spotify in 2014 started a worldwide conversation about streaming and how artists get paid.

584

Her surprise releases of Folklore and Evermore during the pandemic were major events, and both fans and critics praised her creativity.

585

Her influence on social media is huge, with her Tumblr and Instagram posts often creating viral trends and engaging fans.

586

Taylor's Red era helped make the "autumn aesthetic" popular, with fans connecting the album to fall themes like scarves, coffee, and leaves.

587

Her public relationships with celebrities like Joe Jonas, Jake Gyllenhaal, and Harry Styles have been the focus of media attention and have inspired hit songs.

588

Taylor's use of Easter eggs and hidden messages in her music videos has inspired fans to decode every little detail.

590

Taylor's support for other female artists, including collaborations with Haim and Little Big Town, has promoted female empowerment in the music industry.

589

Her decision to write about personal heartbreak in songs like "All Too Well" has inspired many songwriters to be more open and vulnerable in their music.

591

She has inspired a passionate fanbase called "Swifties," who have become one of the most dedicated and organized fan communities in music.

592

Taylor's interactions with fans on social media, like liking their posts and responding to their comments, have helped create a special connection with them.

593

Her Folklore and Evermore albums helped bring indie folk and alternative sounds back into the spotlight in mainstream music.

25

Taylor's Songwriting and Lyricism

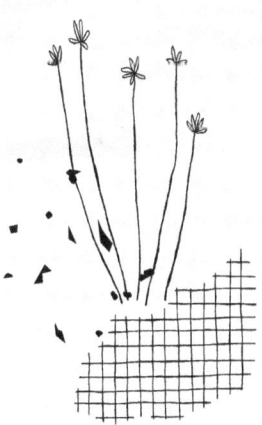

594

Taylor wrote all the songs on her Speak Now album by herself, showing her talent as a solo songwriter.

596

Taylor's song "All Too Well" is thought by many fans and critics to be one of the best breakup songs ever written.

595

She often writes songs based on her own life, using real experiences to tell her stories.

597

She likes to use specific details in her lyrics, like dates, colors, and places, to make the stories feel more real and personal.

598

Taylor has said that songwriting helps her deal with her emotions, almost like therapy.

599

In the song "Enchanted" from Speak Now, there is a hidden message spelling "ADORE," which fans believe is about Owl City's Adam Young.

600

Her song "The Archer" from Lover is about feeling vulnerable and thinking deeply about herself.

601

Taylor often writes songs from other people's points of view, like she did with "Betty" and "The Last Great American Dynasty."

602

The song "Soon You'll Get Better" from Lover is about her mom's fight with cancer, making it one of her most personal songs.

603

Taylor's lyrics are known for clever wordplay and metaphors, like in "Blank Space," where she makes fun of her media image.

604

The line "I once believed love would be burning red, but it's golden" from "Daylight" shows how her view of love has changed over time.

605

Her song "Delicate" talks about feeling unsure and insecure in a new relationship.

606

In "The Lakes" from Folklore, she uses poetic language to talk about wanting a peaceful escape from fame.

607

The lyric "And I can go anywhere I want, anywhere I want, just not home" from "My Tears Ricochet" reflects feelings of loneliness.

608

Her song "New Romantics" is seen as an anthem for her generation, capturing the fun but complicated nature of love and life today.

609

Taylor is known for hiding secret messages in her album notes, where capital letters in the lyrics spell out hidden meanings.

610

Her song "Exile" with Bon Iver from Folklore is written as a conversation between two ex-lovers, which connects deeply with fans.

611

"Invisible String" from Folklore is filled with ideas about fate and destiny, showing her belief in meaningful connections.

612

The lyric "We never painted by the numbers, baby" from "Cornelia Street" is a metaphor for a relationship that didn't follow the usual rules.

26

Behind the Scenes of Album Creation

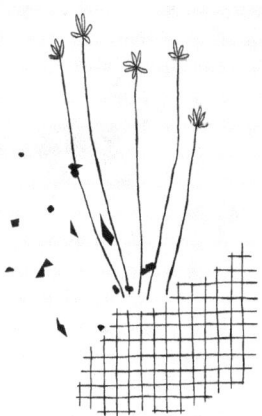

613

Taylor wrote much of Folklore and Evermore while she was in isolation during the COVID-19 pandemic, working remotely with producers Jack Antonoff and Aaron Dessner.

614

The recording process for Fearless took one year, and Taylor wrote many of the songs while she was on tour.

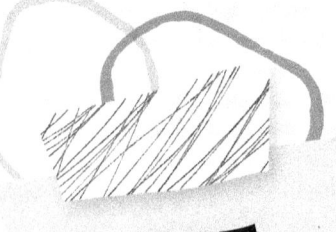

615

1989 was inspired by 1980s pop music, and Taylor has said she listened to artists like Annie Lennox and Madonna while making the album.

616

Taylor wrote Red after a major breakup, and the album reflects many different emotions, from sadness to hope.

617

The Reputation album was influenced by how the media portrayed Taylor, and she used the album to take back control of her story.

618

Taylor often starts writing songs with just one lyric or melody, then builds it into a full song.

619

While making Lover, Taylor was inspired by the idea of love and romance, which is shown in the album's bright, happy style.

620

The Speak Now album was recorded in Nashville, and many of the songs have traditional country music instruments.

621

Taylor decided to re-record her older albums (Taylor's Version) after her original recordings were sold without her permission.

622

The Evermore album was a surprise release that Taylor called the "sister album" to Folklore.

623

Many songs on Red (Taylor's Version) were re-recorded to sound like the originals, but Taylor added new production to give them a fresh feel.

624

Taylor worked with Swedish producer Max Martin on several songs for 1989, including the hits "Shake It Off" and "Blank Space."

625

The song "Betty" from Folklore was inspired by Taylor's friends Blake Lively and Ryan Reynolds, and she used their children's names in the song.

626

Taylor's voice on Reputation was meant to sound more raw and powerful, matching the album's darker themes.

627 ★

The Lover album includes a mix of pop, indie, and synth-pop, showing how Taylor's musical style is always changing.

628

Taylor said she felt very free while making Evermore, focusing more on telling stories than on making it a big commercial success.

629

While re-recording Fearless (Taylor's Version), Taylor made small changes to her vocals to show how much she has grown as an artist.

631

Taylor recorded much of Reputation in secret, and the release of the album was a surprise until she dropped the lead single, "Look What You Made Me Do."

630

1989 was Taylor's first album to completely move away from country music and embrace pop, a decision that was both praised and questioned.

632

Taylor has said that working with Jack Antonoff has been one of her most rewarding partnerships, and he has co-produced many of her recent albums.

27

Taylor's Acting Career

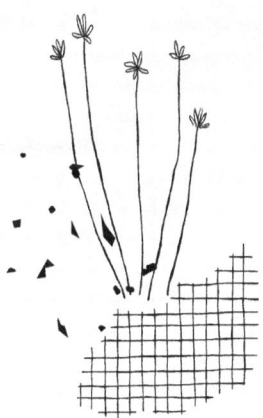

633

Taylor made her acting debut in the 2009 movie Valentine's Day, where she played a cheerful high school student named Felicia.

634

She voiced the character Audrey in the animated movie The Lorax, which is based on the famous Dr. Seuss book.

635

Taylor had a guest role on CSI: Crime Scene Investigation, playing a troubled teenager named Haley Jones.

636

She appears as herself in an episode of New Girl, where she interrupts a wedding to declare her love for one of the characters.

637

Taylor played Bombalurina in the 2019 movie adaptation of the musical Cats.

638

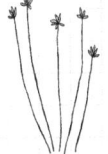

Her performance of the song "Macavity" in Cats was praised for its energy, even though the movie got mixed reviews.

639

Taylor appeared as Rosemary in The Giver, a movie based on the classic book, where she had a small but important role.

640

Taylor has said she loves acting and would be open to doing more film roles in the future.

641

In Miss Americana, a Netflix documentary about her life, Taylor gave fans a close look at her personal and work struggles.

642

Taylor's music has been featured in many movies, including The Hunger Games soundtrack, where she sang the haunting ballad "Safe & Sound."

643

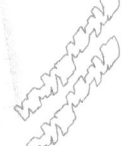

She performed her song "Today Was a Fairytale" for the Valentine's Day movie soundtrack, and it became a hit single.

644

Taylor played herself in a guest appearance on the TV show Hannah Montana, where she performed her song "Crazier."

645

She has been offered many lead roles in Hollywood movies but has been picky about which ones to accept.

646

Taylor received praise for her role in The Giver, with critics saying she brought depth to her character's scenes.

647

She has said that she enjoys the creative challenge of acting but feels most comfortable in the music industry.

648

Taylor was considered for the role of Eponine in Les Misérables, but the part went to actress Samantha Barks.

649

In Miss Americana, Taylor talks about the pressures of fame, politics, and her fight for control over her music.

650

Her role in Cats was her first time working on a major musical, and she trained hard for the singing and dancing parts.

651

Taylor has hosted Saturday Night Live and performed as the musical guest several times, showing her acting skills in funny sketches.

652

She has hinted that she would like to try more serious acting roles in the future, possibly in indie films or theater.

28

Taylor's
Global Reach

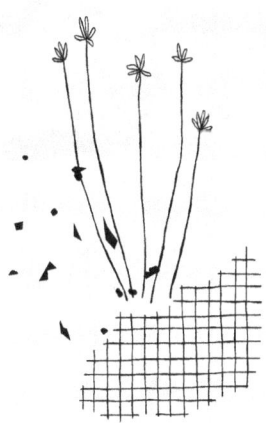

653

Taylor's 1989 World Tour made over $199 million, making it one of the most successful tours ever.

654

She has performed in more than 50 countries across five continents, reaching millions of fans around the world.

655

Taylor's albums are always top-sellers in countries like Japan, the UK, and Australia, showing her global popularity.

656

Taylor has a huge fan base in Latin America, where she sold out shows during her Reputation and 1989 world tours.

657

Her Red and 1989 albums were very successful in the UK, where they both reached number one on the UK Albums Chart.

658

Taylor's influence on fashion is worldwide, with her street style being copied by fans in many different countries.

659

She has worked with international artists, like British singer Zayn Malik on the song "I Don't Wanna Live Forever."

660

Taylor's charity work includes helping with international disaster relief, like when she donated to help after the 2015 earthquake in Nepal.

661

She is one of the few artists to achieve global superstardom while still keeping a close connection with her fans, no matter where they are.

663

She has a large fan base in Asia, where she performed sold-out shows in cities like Tokyo, Singapore, and Shanghai during her world tours.

662

Her music videos have been filmed in different countries, including Africa (Wildest Dreams), New Zealand (Out of the Woods) and Japan (End Game).

664

Taylor's influence on pop culture is global, inspiring fans and artists in places like Brazil, South Korea, and India.

665

Her song "Safe & Sound" from The Hunger Games soundtrack reached number one on the iTunes charts in over 15 countries when it was released.

666

Taylor's global fanbase, called "Swifties," stretches across North America, Europe, Asia, South America, and beyond.

667

She has won international awards, including Brit Awards for Best International Female Solo Artist.

668

Taylor's albums often top the charts in countries like Ireland, France, and Germany, proving her status as a global pop icon.

669

Her Lover album went platinum in many countries, including Canada, Brazil, and Australia.

670

Taylor's global reach grew even more with collaborations on songs like "End Game," which featured Ed Sheeran and rapper Future.

29

Fan Theories and Interpretations

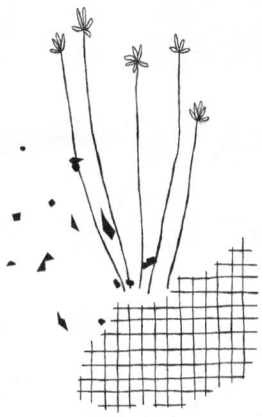

671

One of the most popular fan theories is that the scarf mentioned in "All Too Well" represents lost innocence or a symbol of a past relationship.

672

Fans have guessed that the song "The Last Great American Dynasty" from Folklore is partly about Taylor's own life, comparing her to Rebekah Harkness.

673

The characters James, Betty, and Inez from Folklore are thought to be part of a love triangle, and fans have tried to figure out their relationships through the lyrics.

674

Many fans believe that Taylor's song "Daylight" marks the end of her Red era and shows her more positive view of love and life.

675

The lyric "I'll be the actress starring in your bad dreams" from "Look What You Made Me Do" is seen as a reference to her public feud with Kanye West and Kim Kardashian.

676

Taylor loves to leave Easter eggs, and fans closely watch her social media posts for clues about new music, including hidden numbers, colors, and symbols.

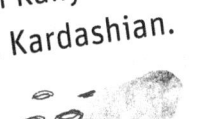

677

Fans think that the lyric "I once was poison ivy, but now I'm your daisy" from "Call It What You Want" shows Taylor's personal change and growth.

678

The color blue in the Lover album artwork and videos is believed to symbolize peace and calm in Taylor's current relationship.

679

Fans have long guessed that Taylor's re-recorded albums would include hidden messages about her battle with Scooter Braun over her master recordings.

680

The music video for "The Man" is full of hidden details, and fans have analyzed the exaggerated male behavior Taylor acts out in the video.

681

Fans believe the mention of "gold" in Lover is Taylor's way of describing true, lasting love compared to the fiery passion in Red.

682

Taylor's song "Invisible String" from Folklore is often seen as a reflection of fate, suggesting that people are brought together by destiny, like soulmates.

683

Many fans believe that "William Bowery," credited as a co-writer on some songs from Folklore, is actually a pseudonym for her boyfriend, Joe Alwyn.

684

In the "Look What You Made Me Do" video, the clock shows 4:16, and fans have speculated whether the time has special meaning about Taylor's life or career.

685

Fans have noticed that Taylor often uses numbers in her lyrics and videos, leading to theories about how numerology influences her songwriting.

686

Many fans believe that the wolves in the "Out of the Woods" music video represent Taylor breaking free from her fears and growing as a person.

687

The idea that the word "clean" in the song "Clean" represents emotional clarity and the end of a toxic relationship is one of the most widely accepted fan interpretations.

688

Fans think Taylor uses certain flowers, like daisies and lavender, in her songs to symbolize innocence, new beginnings, or peace.

30

Iconic Fashion Moments

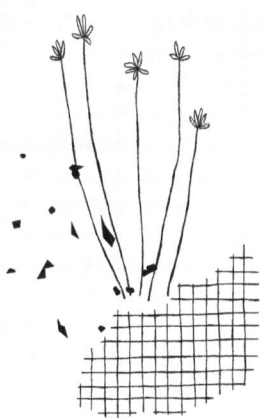

689

At the 2016 Met Gala, Taylor wore a silver metallic mini-dress by Louis Vuitton, which had a futuristic look.

690

During the 1989 era, she had a bold, sleek bob haircut that became one of her most iconic styles.

691

Taylor wore a beautiful pastel Versace gown to the 2021 Grammys, where she won Album of the Year for Folklore.

692

Her Fearless era was known for her glittery dresses and cowboy boots, a look that became her signature country-pop style.

693

In New York, Taylor often wears high-waisted skirts and crop tops, giving her a casual yet polished street style.

694

At the 2014 VMAs, she wore a blue playsuit by Mary Katrantzou, marking her shift from country to pop music.

695

At the 2022 MTV VMAs, Taylor stunned in a custom Oscar de la Renta gown covered in silver crystals with a high slit.

696

For the 2013 ACM Awards, Taylor wore a dramatic Dolce & Gabbana gown with detailed gold embroidery, showing off her evolving style.

697

Her classic red lipstick became a big part of her look during the Red era, representing both the album and her personal style.

698

At the 2015 Met Gala, Taylor wore a a pale pink Calvin Klein Collection gown.

699

In the "You Need to Calm Down" music video, she wore several colorful outfits, including a pink fur coat and heart-shaped sunglasses.

700

At the 2019 Time 100 Gala, where she was honored as one of the most influential people in the world, Taylor wore a floral Etro gown.

701

For her 2018 AMAs performance, Taylor wore a gold sequined bodysuit with thigh-high boots, bringing back a glam pop style.

703

For her Reputation Stadium Tour, Taylor wore a custom black sequined hoodie with snake designs, reflecting the darker themes of the album.

702

During her Folklore era, Taylor embraced the cottagecore style, often seen in cozy cardigans, soft sweaters, and flowy dresses.

704

At the 2019 Billboard Music Awards, she wore a lilac ruffled dress by Raisa & Vanessa, giving off a dreamy and whimsical vibe.

705

During her Red era, Taylor was known for wearing laid-back sweaters and hats, which created a warm and nostalgic feel.

707

For her 2013 Red Tour, Taylor wore vintage-inspired dresses, often with lace, velvet, and deep colors.

706

Her 1989 World Tour featured custom sequined bodysuits and jackets designed by Joseph Cassell, which became a staple of her tour outfits.

708

At the 2021 Brit Awards, Taylor wore a white crop top and matching skirt by Miu Miu, creating a sleek and modern look that highlighted her minimalist style.

31

Taylor's Relationships with Other Artists

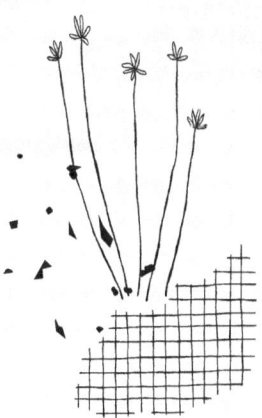

709

Taylor and Halsey
admire each other's
music, and they have
become close friends
in recent years.

710

Taylor has spoken about
how much she looks up
to Beyoncé, especially
after Beyoncé supported
her during the 2009
VMAs controversy.

711

She worked with Justin Vernon
of Bon Iver on "Exile" from
Folklore, and their different
singing styles were loved
by fans and critics.

712

Taylor and Troye Sivan
surprised fans by
performing "My My My!"
together during her
Reputation Stadium Tour.

713

She sang with Stevie Nicks at the 2010 Grammy Awards, performing a mix of Taylor's hit "You Belong with Me" and Fleetwood Mac's "Rhiannon."

715

She wrote "Babe" for the country group Sugarland, and it became a big hit for them.

714

Taylor's partnership with Jack Antonoff has been one of her best, with Antonoff co-writing and producing many of her popular songs.

716

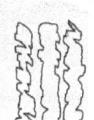

She has had a long friendship with country star Keith Urban, and they have performed together many times.

717

Taylor worked with Ryan Tedder of OneRepublic, who co-wrote and produced "Welcome to New York" and "I Know Places" from 1989.

719

She worked with The Civil Wars for The Hunger Games soundtrack, and their song "Safe & Sound" got a lot of praise.

718

Her collaboration with Phoebe Bridgers on the song "Nothing New" for Red (Taylor's Version) was a standout, mixing their folk styles.

720

Taylor and Olivia Rodrigo have shown public support for each other, with Taylor complimenting Olivia's songwriting.

☆ **721**

She wrote "Better Man" for the country group Little Big Town, and the song became a huge success.

722

Taylor and Katy Perry ended their feud in 2019, and Katy appeared in Taylor's "You Need to Calm Down" music video.

☆ **723**

She worked with rapper Kendrick Lamar on the "Bad Blood" remix, which became a huge hit and won a Grammy Award.

32

Behind the Scenes of Her Tours

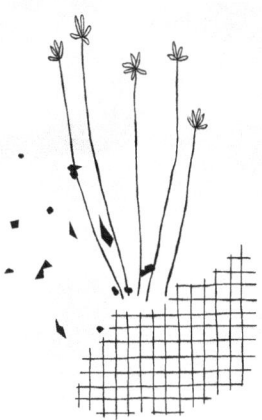

724

Taylor carefully chooses the setlist for each tour, making sure to include fan-favorite songs and surprise songs that fans don't expect.

726

The Speak Now World Tour had a theatrical and fairy-tale-like set design with fireworks and rotating platforms.

725

During her 1989 World Tour, Taylor invited fans backstage after each show for a special meet-and-greet called "Loft '89."

727

For her Red Tour, Taylor designed a floating platform that let her perform above the audience, making her closer to fans in every seat.

728

The Reputation Stadium Tour featured a giant 63-foot inflatable cobra named "Karyn," which was a nod to the snake theme of the album.

729

Taylor often practices for months before a tour to make sure every part, from dancing to singing, is perfect.

730

Her tours are known for their amazing production, with lots of fireworks, cool lighting effects, and giant video screens.

731

Taylor loves to surprise fans with acoustic performances of rare or unreleased songs during her shows, making each concert special.

732

During the Fearless Tour, Taylor would walk through the crowd while singing, creating a more personal experience for fans.

733

The 1989 World Tour had a surprise guest performer at almost every show, from celebrities like Julia Roberts to musicians like Steven Tyler.

734

Taylor helps design her custom costumes for each tour, working closely with designers to make sure the outfits match the themes of her albums.

735

For her Reputation Tour, Taylor's team created wristbands for everyone in the audience that lit up in sync with the music and light show.

736

She often brings out her family and close friends for special moments during her concerts, making her shows feel more personal.

737

Her Fearless Tour was the first time she performed in big arenas, marking a major moment in her career as a headliner.

738

Taylor has said that she likes to change up the arrangements of her songs for live performances, giving fans a new version of songs they know.

739

The Red Tour featured a circus-themed performance of "We Are Never Ever Getting Back Together," with backup dancers dressed in colorful outfits.

740

Taylor always includes an acoustic segment in her concerts, where she sings a different song at each stop of the tour.

741

During the Speak Now World Tour, Taylor played several instruments on stage, including piano, banjo, and guitar, showing her musical skills.

742

The Reputation Stadium Tour had impressive visuals, with video screens showing snake images and dystopian landscapes.

33

Taylor's Inspirations and Influences

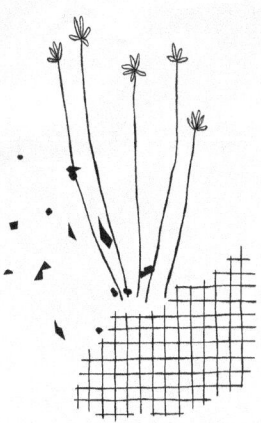

743

Taylor has said that Shania Twain is one of her biggest musical influences, especially for blending country and pop music.

744

She admires Paul McCartney for how he balances his personal and professional life, something Taylor hopes to do as well.

745

Taylor is inspired by classic rock artists like Bruce Springsteen, whom she looks up to for their storytelling in music.

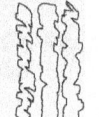

746

She has mentioned that Joni Mitchell's Blue album was a big influence on her own songwriting, especially for its emotional honesty.

747

She has praised Carole King as an inspiration, especially for writing timeless songs that people from all generations love.

748

Taylor's switch to pop with 1989 was inspired by 1980s music, with artists like Madonna and Annie Lennox shaping the album's sound.

749

She has said that Patsy Cline's emotional singing and storytelling in country music influenced her early songwriting.

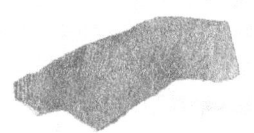

750

Taylor has been influenced by famous writers, including F. Scott Fitzgerald, and has expressed admiration for the novel The Great Gatsby.

751

She has mentioned that James Taylor, who she was named after, was an early influence on her music.

753

Taylor's love for musical theater, especially the works of Andrew Lloyd Webber, led to her decision to act in the movie Cats.

752

Taylor has said that The Dixie Chicks (now known as The Chicks) were a huge inspiration to her when she started her country music career.

754

She has praised Ed Sheeran as one of her biggest musical inspirations and collaborators, saying that they push each other to be more creative.

755

Taylor has said that Leonard Cohen's poetic style of songwriting has been a major influence on her writing.

756

She admires Dolly Parton's storytelling, especially how Dolly mixes humor and emotion in her songs.

757

Taylor's songwriting is also influenced by movies, and she has mentioned that directors like Guillermo del Toro inspire her music videos.

758

She is a fan of J.K. Rowling's Harry Potter series and says the books inspire her belief in the power of storytelling.

759

Taylor has mentioned that Stevie Nicks' mix of rock and mysticism has inspired some of her more experimental work on Folklore.

34

Memorable Awards
Show Moments

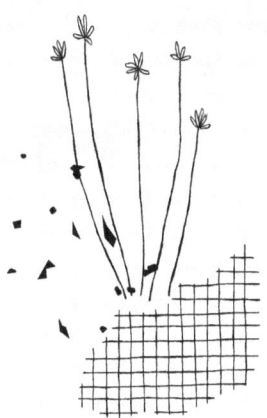

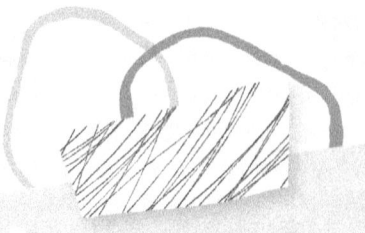

760

Taylor's 2009 VMA moment became one of the most talked-about events in pop culture when Kanye West interrupted her speech for winning "You Belong with Me."

761

At the 2016 Grammy Awards, Taylor used her Album of the Year speech to indirectly respond to Kanye West's controversial lyrics about her.

762

Taylor made history as the first woman to win Album of the Year three times at the Grammys when she won for Folklore in 2021.

763

At the 2014 American Music Awards, Taylor performed "Blank Space" live on TV for the first time, earning a standing ovation.

764

During the 2013 VMAs, Taylor gave a shoutout to her ex-boyfriend when she accepted the Best Female Video award for "I Knew You Were Trouble."

766

At the 2018 Billboard Music Awards, Taylor won Top Female Artist, making a big return to award shows.

765

In 2021, Taylor performed an emotional version of "All Too Well (10-Minute Version)" on Saturday Night Live, marking the first live performance of the extended track.

767

During the 2015 Brit Awards, Taylor performed "Blank Space" with elaborate choreography, making it one of her most memorable live performances in the UK.

768

In 2016, Taylor received the first-ever Taylor Swift Award from BMI, honoring her major influence on songwriting.

770

Taylor made history by accepting the Global Icon Award at the 2021 Brit Awards, the first female artist to receive the honor.

769

At the 2021 Grammy Awards, Taylor performed a medley of songs from Folklore and Evermore on a forest-like stage.

771

At the 2019 MTV VMAs, Taylor opened the show with a performance of "You Need to Calm Down" and "Lover," setting the tone for the night.

772

She accepted the Artist of the Decade Award at the 2019 AMAs with a powerful medley of her biggest hits and a message about artist rights.

773

During the 2009 CMA Awards, Taylor became the youngest artist to win Entertainer of the Year at just 19 years old.

774 ★

Taylor's first big awards show performance was at the 2007 ACM Awards, where she performed "Our Song," helping her rise to fame.

775

At the 2010 Grammys, Taylor performed "You Belong with Me" and "Rhiannon" with Stevie Nicks, a dream collaboration for her.

776

Taylor won her first Grammy Award in 2010 for Best Female Country Vocal Performance with "White Horse."

777

She performed "Mean" at the 2011 Grammy Awards, using the performance to stand up to her critics after receiving harsh reviews.

778

Taylor became the first female artist to perform twice on Saturday Night Live, showing her talent as both a singer and actress.

779

At the 2015 iHeartRadio Music Awards, Taylor won Best Lyrics for "Blank Space," proving her songwriting skills.

35

Taylor's Signature Style

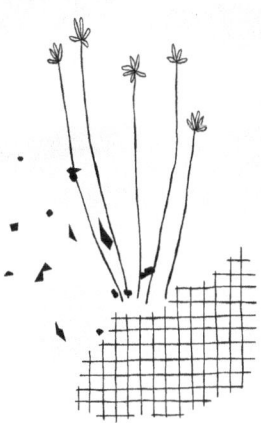

780

During the 1989 era, Taylor's go-to look was high-waisted shorts and striped t-shirts, which influenced many of her fans.

782

Taylor's love for vintage-inspired dresses became a key part of her look during the Speak Now eras.

781

In the Reputation era, she introduced a darker, more dramatic style, often wearing black leather jackets and dark plum shade lipstick.

783

Her Red era was known for her sleek and polished style, with bold red lipstick and preppy coats becoming part of her signature look.

784

During the Lover era, Taylor often wore light, soft colors and simple, fun outfits that matched the bright and romantic feel of the album.

786

Taylor's street style usually includes chic sunglasses, ankle boots, and stylish handbags, making her a fashion icon.

785

In the Reputation era, she often accessorized with snake-themed jewelry and clothing, embracing the snake as part of her rebranding.

787

She loves sparkly, sequined dresses, which were a big part of her 1989 World Tour.

788

Taylor's hairstyle changes have been closely followed by fans, from her country curls to her sleek, blonde bob during the 1989 era.

789

She is known for mixing timeless, classic pieces with more affordable fashion, often blending high-end designer clothes with everyday items.

790

During the Lover era, Taylor wore pastel colors like baby blues, pinks, and lavenders in her casual and formal outfits.

791

Her love for classic cat-eye makeup became a big part of her look during the Red and 1989 eras.

792

Taylor often wears tailored blazers and suits, giving her a polished and professional look for public appearances and interviews.

794

Taylor is known for experimenting with bold nail art, often matching her nail colors with her outfits or album themes.

793

She has been seen in retro-inspired outfits like polka dot dresses and A-line skirts, especially during her early country music years.

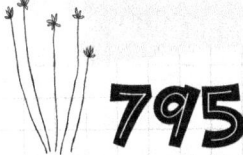

795

During her Folklore and Evermore eras, Taylor embraced a cottagecore style, wearing cozy cardigans, plaid jackets, and flowy dresses.

796

She frequently adds glamour to her casual looks with statement necklaces and earrings.

797

For everyday outfits, Taylor often chooses practical but stylish shoes like ankle boots, ballet flats, and Converse sneakers.

798

Taylor's love of scarves is well-known, especially during her Red era, where she used scarves as both a fashion statement and a symbol in her lyrics.

799

Her love for vintage hairstyles, like soft waves and victory rolls, often adds a retro touch to her red carpet looks.

36

Taylor's Evolution as a Performer

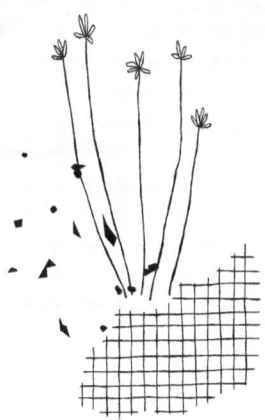

800

Taylor's first big live performance was at the Bluebird Café in Nashville, where she was discovered by Scott Borchetta.

801

During her Fearless Tour, Taylor performed in front of thousands of people, marking her rise from a rising star to a country superstar.

802

Taylor's Speak Now World Tour performances were praised for being theatrical, with fancy sets and many costume changes.

803

She started adding choreographed dance routines to her performances during the 1989 World Tour, showing her shift into pop music.

☆ 804

Taylor's confidence on stage has grown over time, and her Reputation Stadium Tour showed her as a powerful and fearless performer.

805

Her acoustic performances during tours like Red and Reputation highlight her raw vocal talent and her ability to connect emotionally with fans.

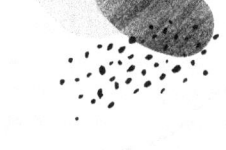

806

Taylor's live shows often feature longer versions of her songs, where she adds new lyrics or instruments to make the performance unique.

☆ 807

She is known for telling stories during live performances, often sharing personal stories before singing, which helps her connect with the audience.

808

During her 1989 World Tour, Taylor included high-energy dance numbers and dramatic set designs, showing her growth as a full pop performer.

809

Taylor's stage presence is known for being friendly and relatable, with many fans saying she makes even big stadiums feel personal.

810

During the Reputation Stadium Tour, Taylor performed difficult dance routines while singing live, showing her versatility as an entertainer.

811

She likes to experiment with different musical arrangements in her live shows, giving her songs a fresh sound every time.

812

Taylor's reputation as a live performer is strengthened by her attention to detail, from the lighting to the dance routines and set designs.

813

She is respected in the industry for seamlessly switching between playing instruments, like guitar and piano, during her live performances.

814

Taylor's Fearless Tour included a memorable performance of "Love Story," where she was lifted into the air on a balcony set, creating a magical moment for fans.

815

She is praised for connecting with her audience during performances, often acknowledging specific fans in the crowd by name or signs they hold up.

816

Taylor's performances of "All Too Well" have become legendary among her fans, and the 10-minute version is one of the most anticipated live moments.

817

Taylor's concert setlists often include a mix of her biggest hits and lesser-known songs, making them fun for both casual listeners and her biggest fans.

818

Her ability to sing with control while performing complex dance routines has impressed critics and fans, especially during her Reputation and 1989 tours.

37

Taylor's Views on Life

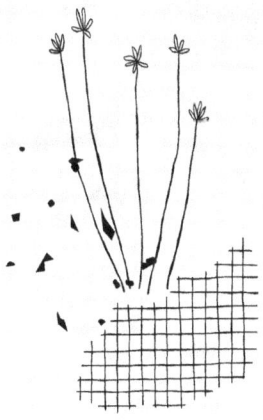

819

Taylor grew up in a Christian household, and her family and life experiences have shaped how she looks at life and her sense of responsibility.

820

She has publicly spoken out for marriage equality and uses her platform to fight against discrimination.

821

In 2019, Taylor supported political candidates for the first time, backing Democratic candidates in Tennessee and encouraging her fans to vote.

822

Taylor believes in equality for everyone, no matter their gender, race, or sexual orientation, and she uses her voice to support progressive causes.

823

Her song "The Man" from Lover talks about the double standards women face, showing her feminist views and support for gender equality.

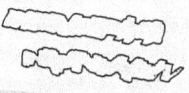

824

Taylor has donated to many causes, including disaster relief, hunger, and education, showing her belief in giving back to society.

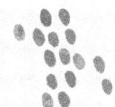

825

Taylor strongly believes in the power of self-reinvention and embraces change as an important and positive part of life.

826

She believes artists should have control over their own work and has fought for musicians' rights, inspired by her own fight to regain control of her masters.

827

In her 2020 Netflix documentary Miss Americana, Taylor shared her journey to finding her political voice, admitting that she once stayed away from politics to avoid losing fans.

829

She has spoken about her belief in personal growth and that life is a journey of learning and self-improvement.

828

Taylor's belief in standing up for what's right led her to write an open letter to Apple Music in 2015, which led to the company changing how they paid artists.

830

She often talks about the importance of mental health and believes in taking care of emotional well-being, a theme she explores in songs like "The Archer."

831

Taylor's songs often show her thoughts about love, loss, and personal strength, as seen in songs like "Daylight" and "Clean," which focus on self-reflection and healing.

833

Taylor cares about protecting the environment and has supported different environmental causes, donating to groups that focus on conservation.

832

She has been critical of how the media and society place unfair expectations on women, using her platform to challenge beauty standards and stereotypes.

834

Her song "Only the Young" was written in response to political frustration and encourages young people to get involved and shape the future.

38

Taylor's Dreams and Aspirations

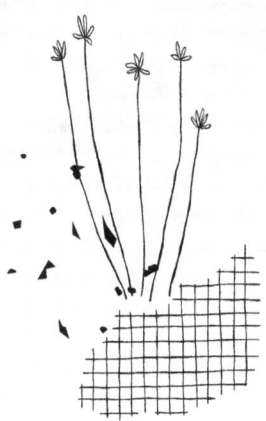

835

Taylor has said she dreams of one-day writing and directing her own movie, combining her love of music and storytelling on the big screen.

836

She wants to keep re-recording her earlier albums (Taylor's Version) so she can fully own her music.

837

Taylor has shown a strong interest in mentoring and supporting young, new artists.

838

She hopes to keep growing as a songwriter and wants to explore new music genres and themes as she changes and evolves.

839

Taylor has mentioned she'd love to write a novel someday, inspired by her love of reading and telling stories.

840

One of her dreams is to perform in more intimate settings, like small acoustic shows or "secret" performances for her fans.

841

Taylor dreams of getting more involved in philanthropy, especially supporting causes like education and helping artists.

842

Taylor hopes to one day release a book with her lyrics and songwriting notes, giving fans a closer look at her creative process.

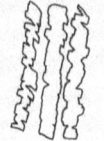

843

She's mentioned that one of her dreams is to balance her personal life and career, wanting to feel normal despite her fame.

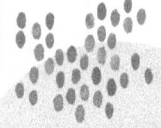

844

Taylor wants to travel the world more and dreams of performing in new, faraway places.

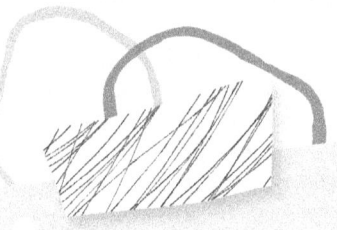

845

She has shown interest in writing music for Broadway and hopes to create a musical based on her life or songs.

846

She is passionate about fighting for artists' rights and dreams of helping other musicians own their work.

847

One of her goals is to create more community-focused experiences for her fans, like her "Secret Sessions," where she connects with them directly.

849

Taylor has said she wants to explore different art forms, like photography and painting, as creative outlets beyond music.

848

She dreams of winning an Oscar for Best Original Song, possibly for a song she writes for a movie she's involved in.

850

She dreams of leaving a lasting legacy, where her music continues to inspire future generations of musicians and songwriters.

39

Taylor's
Relationships

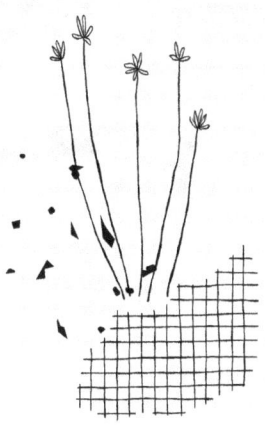

851

She dated Joe Jonas in 2008, and their breakup led her to write the song "Forever & Always."

852

Taylor was linked to Taylor Lautner after they met on the set of the movie Valentine's Day, and she wrote "Back to December" about him.

853

In 2009, Taylor briefly dated John Mayer, and their relationship inspired the song "Dear John."

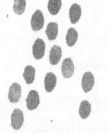

854

She dated Jake Gyllenhaal in 2010, and her heartbreak from that relationship is believed to have inspired songs like "All Too Well."

855

In 2012, Taylor was in a relationship with Conor Kennedy, who is part of the famous Kennedy family.

856

Taylor's relationship with Harry Styles in 2012 became one of her most famous romances, with songs like "Style" and "Out of the Woods" rumored to be about him.

857

She briefly dated British actor Tom Hiddleston in 2016, and their relationship attracted a lot of media attention.

858

Taylor's song "We Are Never Ever Getting Back Together" is believed to be about one of her former boyfriends, possibly Jake Gyllenhaal.

859

Her relationship with Calvin Harris, a famous DJ, lasted for over a year before they broke up in 2016.

861

She often writes about the highs and lows of love, from the excitement of a new romance to the pain of a breakup.

860

Taylor has said that she uses her music as a way to process her feelings about love and relationships.

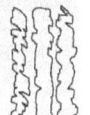

862

In 2017, Taylor started dating British actor Joe Alwyn, and many of Taylor's fans believe that her song "Gorgeous" is about Joe Alwyn.

863

Taylor and Joe Alwyn have co-written several songs together, including tracks on her albums Folklore and Evermore.

865

Her song "Lover" is thought to be a tribute to her relationship with Joe Alwyn, celebrating their love.

864

Taylor's relationship with Joe Alwyn is considered one of her most stable and long-lasting romances.

866

Taylor's love life has been the subject of much speculation, but she has said that she writes from her own experiences and feelings.

867

Many of Taylor's fans appreciate how open she is about her emotions in her songs, especially when it comes to love.

869

She once said in an interview that she writes about love because it's something everyone can relate to.

868

Her song "Begin Again" is about finding hope and love again after a breakup.

870

Taylor's song "The 1" from Folklore is believed to be about reflecting on a past relationship that didn't work out.

871

Despite the media attention, Taylor has said she values privacy in her relationships, especially when she was with Joe Alwyn.

873

Many fans believe that Taylor's Reputation album was partly inspired by the media's portrayal of her love life.

872

Her song "Cornelia Street" is thought to be about her relationship with Joe Alwyn and the time they spent together in New York.

874

Taylor and NFL star Travis Kelce have been recently linked, creating a lot of excitement among fans and the media.

875

While Taylor hasn't talked about specific plans for marriage, she has expressed hopes of finding a stable and happy personal life.

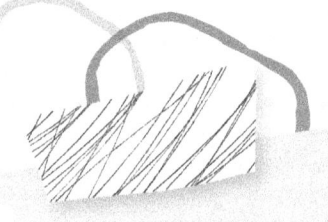

876

Her song "Lover" talks about deep, committed love, and many fans think it reflects her hopes for the future.

40

Secret Facts Only a Few People Know

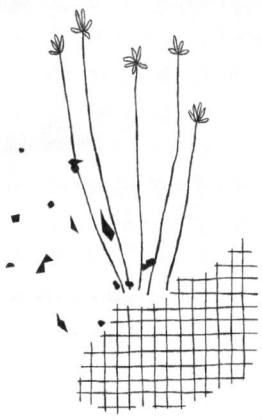

877

Ed Sheeran has a "Red" tattoo, symbolizing his friendship with Taylor and the tour they did together.

878

Taylor's lucky number 13 appears in various hidden ways in her music videos, stage designs, and even in her social media posts.

879

During her 1989 tour, Taylor personally handpicked the surprise guests who joined her on stage based on her admiration for their work.

880

Taylor used to hide messages in the liner notes of her albums, with capitalized letters in the lyrics that spelled out hidden meanings related to the songs.

881

Taylor's songwriting pseudonym is "Nils Sjöberg," which she used to co-write Calvin Harris's hit "This Is What You Came For."

882

The perfume Taylor wore while recording Red was Marc Jacobs' "Daisy," and she wore it so much during that time that she now associates the smell with the album.

883

Taylor once snuck into a theater to watch The Hunger Games when her song "Safe & Sound" was playing during the movie.

884

Her personal favorite song from her catalog changes frequently, but she once revealed in an interview that "All Too Well" is one of the most emotionally significant to her.

885

Taylor has handwritten letters from both Joni Mitchell and Paul McCartney framed in her home as treasured mementos.

886

One of her secret indulgences is making midnight trips to fast-food chains like In-N-Out Burger with her friends.

887

Taylor's mother, Andrea, is a huge influence on her fashion choices and often helps her decide what to wear for big events.

888

She has a private Tumblr account where she follows fan theories and interacts anonymously with Swifties.

889

Taylor always carries a notebook with her, just in case she gets inspired to write lyrics while she's out and about.

890

She is an avid Scrabble player and has been known to play intense games with her friends and family during holidays.

891

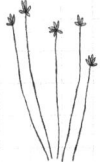

Taylor's favorite midnight snack is buttered toast with cinnamon and sugar.

892

Taylor is a huge fan of Friends and has had multiple cast members as guests at her concerts.

893

Taylor is so good at picking out Easter eggs and hidden references that she's been invited to consult on movie scripts for hidden clues and surprises.

894

Taylor has a "TAS" monogram (for Taylor Alison Swift) embroidered on many of her custom tour costumes.

895

She once revealed that she sleeps with her cats in her bed and even has special steps so they can climb up comfortably.

896

Taylor is a big fan of the board game Settlers of Catan and often hosts game nights with her close friends.

897 ♪

She sends personal gifts to her backup dancers and band members during holidays, thanking them for their hard work on tour.

899

Taylor has a secret room in her Rhode Island mansion filled with personal items and memorabilia from every era of her career.

898

Her song "Clean" from 1989 was inspired by a conversation she had while walking through London in the rain.

900

She is known to have handwritten multiple versions of certain song lyrics before deciding on the final version, with drafts kept in her journals.

901

Taylor once took her entire tour crew on vacation to Hawaii as a thank-you after the 1989 World Tour.

902

She has a personal photographer who travels with her on tour to capture behind-the-scenes moments that she keeps private.

903

Taylor owns a vintage Polaroid camera collection and uses them to document special moments with her friends and family.

904

Taylor loves classic literature and has read Pride and Prejudice multiple times, which is why she references it in her song "Love Story."

905

She has a hidden "studio" playlist of her favorite songs to listen to while she's recording new music, which includes artists like Fleetwood Mac and The National.

906

Taylor has an extensive collection of rare vinyl records, including original pressings of iconic albums like Rumours and Abbey Road.

907

She once designed a series of friendship bracelets for her closest friends, inspired by the ones her fans make and trade at her concerts.

908

Taylor has her own line of custom guitars made by Taylor Guitars, each engraved with her name and personal designs.

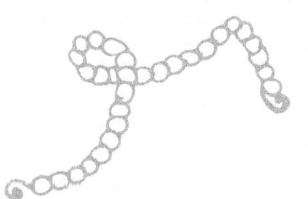
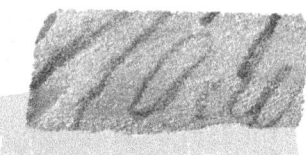

909

She and Blake Lively have a tradition of sending each other funny voice messages throughout the day to keep in touch.

910

Taylor personally selects the candles used in her tour dressing rooms, with her favorite scent being vanilla lavender.

911

She's a fan of crossword puzzles and has been known to start her mornings by completing them over coffee before heading into the studio.

912

Taylor's favorite drink is a lavender latte, and she often orders it when she's working on new music.

913

She secretly auditioned for the role of Éponine in Les Misérables, but ultimately didn't get the part.

915

Despite her polished image, Taylor has a huge love for horror movies and regularly hosts horror movie marathons with her friends.

914

Taylor has a secret vault where she keeps original, unreleased songs that have never been heard by the public.

916

She learned to drive in a Toyota Land Cruiser on her family's farm in Pennsylvania.

917

Taylor is allergic to horses, despite having grown up on a Christmas tree farm with lots of animals.

918

She once sent an anonymous donation to a school in Nashville to help fund their music program but never took credit for it.

919

Taylor has written songs under a male pseudonym for other artists, but she's never revealed all the songs she's worked on anonymously.

920

She used to prank call her friends when she was younger and still loves pulling elaborate pranks on her team while on tour.

921

Taylor's personal "relaxation room" in her house is filled with bookshelves, soft blankets, and a soundproof door, which she uses to decompress.

922

Taylor loves Halloween, and she goes all out with elaborate costumes and decorations at her homes.

923

She once bought a car as a surprise gift for a childhood friend who was going through financial difficulties.

924

Taylor has a passion for cooking and once considered releasing a cookbook featuring her favorite recipes, but she never went through with it.

925

She secretly bought out entire cinemas for her and her friends to watch movies in private after getting mobbed by paparazzi.

926

Taylor knows how to play over five instruments, including guitar, piano, banjo, ukulele, and violin.

927

Taylor has never had a "ghostwriter" and is fiercely protective of writing every single word of her songs herself.

928

She once went undercover at a fan's Taylor Swift-themed party by wearing a disguise, only revealing herself at the end of the event.

929

Taylor has a fear of sea urchins after stepping on one as a child while on vacation.

930

She's been known to write songs at 3 a.m. when she can't sleep, with some of her biggest hits being penned during late-night writing sessions.

931

Taylor keeps a "vision board" in her home studio where she pins images and phrases that inspire her for upcoming projects.

932

She once purchased a painting for $1 million at a charity auction to help fund art programs for children.

933

Taylor wrote a song about her childhood friends but has never released it, keeping it as a personal tribute to her early years.

934

She used to knit scarves and sweaters for her cats when she first adopted them, and she continues knitting for relaxation.

935

Taylor is incredibly good at archery and often practices it as a hobby, even setting up targets at her homes.

936

She has a secret collection of awards that she keeps in a locked room, preferring not to showcase them publicly.

937

Taylor often carries a small notebook to jot down random thoughts or song ideas when inspiration strikes, even during casual conversations.

938

She can't swim very well and has admitted in interviews that she's not comfortable being in deep water.

939

Taylor once had a dream about a song melody and woke up in the middle of the night to record it on her phone, later turning it into one of her hit singles.

940

She's secretly a gamer and enjoys playing video games like The Sims and Animal Crossing when she's relaxing at home.

41

Easter Eggs
in Taylor's Music

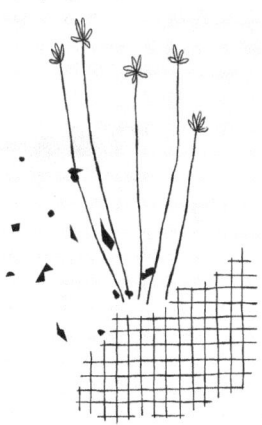

941

In "The Last Great American Dynasty," the story of Rebekah Harkness is similar to Taylor's own life, with the media and fans being obsessed with her personal life.

942

In the Fearless album, the line "You gave me roses, and I left them there to die" in "White Horse" is a nod to the roses in her song "Love Story."

943

The background singing in "The Archer" reminds fans of "All You Had to Do Was Stay" from 1989, connecting both songs with themes of feeling vulnerable.

944

In Red (Taylor's Version), Taylor added the song "Ronan," which is a very personal song she wrote for a boy who passed away from cancer. It wasn't in the original Red album.

945

In the "Look What You Made Me Do" music video, Taylor sits in a bathtub of jewels, which refers to how the media called her "greedy" after she won her court case against a DJ.

946

In Folklore, the songs "Betty," "Cardigan," and "August" tell the same love story but from different characters' points of view: Betty, James, and Inez.

947

The cardigan in the "Cardigan" music video is a symbol of memories and lost love, and Taylor gave similar cardigans to her fans as part of the merch.

948

In Lover, the song "Cornelia Street" is named after a street in New York City where Taylor used to live, and it's important because of a relationship that started there.

949

The song "Seven" from Folklore talks about childhood and close bonds, which connects to Taylor's roots in Pennsylvania.

950

In Red (Taylor's Version), the lyrics in the 10-minute version of "All Too Well" mention a "red scarf," which fans think is a symbol of Taylor's relationship with Jake Gyllenhaal.

951

In "Invisible String," the line "Time, curious time" might be about how Taylor believes in fate and how people are connected by time.

952

The three horses in the "Blank Space" music video might represent three of Taylor's past relationships that were talked about in the media.

953

In the 1989 album, the song "Out of the Woods" is about a real snowmobile accident Taylor had with her ex-boyfriend, who people think was Harry Styles.

954

In Folklore and Evermore, Taylor used the name "William Bowery," which is actually her boyfriend Joe Alwyn, who helped write some of the songs.

955

The house in the "Lover" music video shows different stages of Taylor's career, with each room representing a different album era.

956

In the Fearless album, the secret message in the song "The Way I Loved You" says "We Can't Go Back," which may be about a past relationship Taylor regrets.

957

In Red (Taylor's Version), the new song "I Bet You Think About Me" is believed to be about Conor Kennedy, who Taylor dated for a short time.

958

In Reputation, the song "Gorgeous" is thought to be about how Taylor first noticed Joe Alwyn, and how she was struck by how handsome he was.

959

Taylor's favorite number 13 is seen in the "You Belong with Me" video, where the male lead has the number 13 written on his hand.

960

The line "Darling, I'm a nightmare dressed like a daydream" in "Blank Space" is a response to how the media said Taylor was manipulative in relationships.

961

In Lover, the song "Afterglow" talks about making mistakes and fixing them, and some fans think it's about Taylor's relationship with Calvin Harris.

962

Taylor uses colors in her songs to show different feelings. In Lover, the color blue shows calmness, while red in older albums showed passion.

963

The bridge in "Cruel Summer," where Taylor screams, "I love you, ain't that the worst thing you ever heard?" is similar to the emotional bridges in "All Too Well."

964

In Speak Now, the song "Long Live" is Taylor's way of thanking her fans for sticking with her throughout her career.

965

In Lover, the line "I once believed love would be burning red, but it's golden" shows how Taylor now feels more at peace in her relationship with Joe Alwyn.

966

In Reputation, the song "King of My Heart" is believed to be about Joe Alwyn, showing how he made Taylor feel calm after a difficult time.

967

The house in the "Lover" music video was inspired by Wes Anderson movies, especially The Royal Tenenbaums. Each room in the house represents a part of Taylor's life.

968

In Evermore, the song "It's Time to Go" is thought to be about Taylor leaving Big Machine Records and fighting to own her music.

969

Taylor hides song lyrics in her music videos. In "Me!", the word "Lover" is seen on a neon sign, which hints at her album title.

971

In Speak Now, the song "Back to December" is believed to be Taylor apologizing to Taylor Lautner, who she briefly dated.

970

The "golden thread" in the song "Invisible String" is based on a Chinese myth that says a red thread connects two people who are meant to be together.

972

The birdcage in the "Out of the Woods" video shows how Taylor felt trapped by the media attention during her relationship with Harry Styles.

973

The line "My reputation's never been worse, so you must like me for me" in "Delicate" is about how Taylor felt when the media was against her, but someone loved her for who she was.

974

In the "Willow" video, the golden thread is a symbol of the connection between two lovers, which is like the string imagery in "Invisible String."

975

In the "Blank Space" video, Taylor cuts a painting with a knife, which represents how the media said she ruined her past relationships.

976

Taylor's song "Wonderland" from 1989 uses themes from Alice in Wonderland to describe falling in love and losing control.

977

The clock on the Fearless (Taylor's Version) album cover shows 1:13, which is a reference to Taylor's favorite number 13.

979

The bridge in the 10-minute version of "All Too Well" talks about Taylor being left alone at her 21st birthday party, which fans believe was because of Jake Gyllenhaal.

978

In the "Red" music video, Taylor leaves behind a red scarf, which fans think is a symbol of a lost relationship.

980

In Lover, Taylor mentions "daisies," which could show how her Red era was about fiery passion, while Lover is calmer and gentler.

981

In Evermore, the song "Right Where You Left Me" talks about being stuck in a moment of heartbreak, and fans think this is how Taylor felt at certain times in her life.

982

The color green in Folklore is used to show jealousy or unresolved feelings, especially in the song "The 1," which looks at past love versus current happiness.

983

In "This Is Me Trying," the line "Cursed the space that I needed" talks about Taylor's personal struggles with mental health and how she needed time alone to heal.

984

In the Reputation album, Taylor hides the word "delicate" in the background of the music video for the song "... Ready for It?" which hints at the next single.

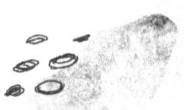

985

In the "Me!" music video, there are 13 clouds in the sky during one scene, which is a nod to Taylor's favorite number.

987

In Folklore, Taylor sings about a "robber" in "Invisible String." This is thought to refer to Joe Alwyn, since he starred in a movie called The Favourite where his character was involved in stealing.

986

The birdcage in the "Begin Again" video symbolizes feeling trapped in a past relationship but finding freedom in a new one.

988

In "Daylight," Taylor sings "I once believed love would be burning red, but it's golden." This is a callback to her Red album and how her view of love has changed.

989

The "King of My Heart" music video shows a crown being put on a girl's head, which fans believe represents Taylor finally finding someone who treats her like royalty.

990

The background vocals in "I Did Something Bad" have a slight echo, making the song feel larger than life, which fits the theme of the Reputation album.

991

In "You Belong With Me," Taylor writes "I Love You" on her hand, which was something she used to do before every show as a good luck charm.

992

In "Look What You Made Me Do," Taylor is dressed as different versions of herself from her past music videos, symbolizing her evolution as an artist.

993

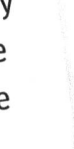

In the Fearless music video for "Love Story," Taylor is wearing a princess gown, which symbolizes the fairy tale love story she sings about in the song.

994

In Red (Taylor's Version), the song "Forever Winter" has hidden references to friendship and mental health struggles that Taylor has supported throughout her career.

995

In Speak Now, the song "Dear John" has guitar solos that are thought to sound like John Mayer's style of playing, a hint about who the song might be about.

996

The tree in the background of the Reputation music video for "Call It What You Want" is decorated with lights, which Taylor used to put on her tree at her parents' house.

997

The lyric "My castle crumbled overnight" in "Call It What You Want" may be a reference to how Taylor's public image was damaged after media controversies.

998

In "Paper Rings" from Lover, Taylor talks about loving someone so much she would marry them with paper rings, which hints at how she cares more about the person than material things.

999

In Fearless, the hidden message in "Hey Stephen" spells out "Love and theft," which is believed to be a reference to the band Love and Theft, who Taylor toured with.

1000

The number "13" is hidden in the shadows of the "Lover" music video, representing Taylor's lucky number and her birthday.

1001

In the "Delicate" music video, Taylor wears a dress that resembles the one she wore to the 2014 Met Gala, which marked a turning point in her style.

1003

In 1989, Taylor uses the phrase "wildest dreams" in the song "I Know Places," a phrase she later turns into a full song in 1989.

1002

In "The Lakes" from Folklore, the lyrics mention "calamitous love" and "red roses," which could refer to Taylor's dramatic love stories in the past.

1004

The lyric "I ask the traffic lights if it'll be alright" in "Death by a Thousand Cuts" was inspired by a scene from the movie Someone Great.

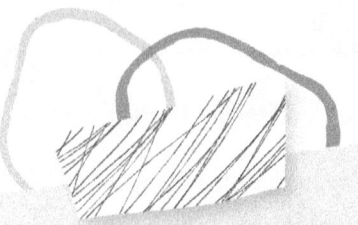

1005

The snake imagery in the Reputation album started as a way to respond to people calling Taylor a snake, but she turned it into a symbol of strength and rebirth.

1006

The clock in the Red music video shows the time 4:15, which could be a subtle nod to April 15th, an important date for Taylor's Fearless tour.

1007

The lyric "I'm shining like fireworks over your sad, empty town" in Speak Now's "Dear John" is about Taylor finding her strength after a difficult breakup.

1008

In "False God," the saxophone plays throughout the song, symbolizing the jazzy, romantic feel of the relationship she's singing about.

1009

The lyrics of "This Love" from 1989 describe a love that comes and goes like the ocean tide, mirroring Taylor's belief that love can be unpredictable.

1010

The "Look What You Made Me Do" music video shows Taylor on a throne of snakes, which represents how she took control of her narrative.

1011

In Evermore, the song "Dorothea" is thought to be about a friend from Taylor's past, and many fans believe the name "Dorothea" is a pseudonym for this person.

1012

In 1989, the song "Out of the Woods" has a line about "twenty stitches in a hospital room," which fans believe is about a snowmobile accident Taylor had with her ex.

1013

The lyric "We were built to fall apart, then fall back together" from 1989's "Out of the Woods" hints at a relationship that was always on and off.

1015

The lyrics of "The Last Time" from Red repeat the words "This is the last time," symbolizing the final end of a rocky relationship.

1014

In "Mirrorball" from Folklore, Taylor compares herself to a disco ball, reflecting how she changes herself to fit in and please others.

1016

In Fearless, Taylor's song "Change" is about staying strong and not giving up, even when things are tough.

1017

In Reputation, the song "Dancing with Our Hands Tied" uses a metaphor about being restricted, reflecting how Taylor felt in her public relationships.

1018

In the "Willow" music video, Taylor follows a magical glowing thread through the forest, symbolizing her journey to find love and happiness.

1019

The lyric "I can still see it all in my mind" in Red's "Holy Ground" reflects on how Taylor remembers special moments in past relationships.

1020

In "Exile" from Folklore, Taylor and Bon Iver's characters sing from different perspectives, showing how each person in a breakup sees the story differently.

1021

In Evermore, "Coney Island" refers to both the amusement park and the ups and downs of a relationship, much like a rollercoaster.

1022

The lyric "You drew stars around my scars" in "Cardigan" shows how Taylor believes love can help heal past emotional wounds.

1023

In "This Is Why We Can't Have Nice Things," Taylor refers to a broken relationship, possibly talking about the loss of trust in a friendship.

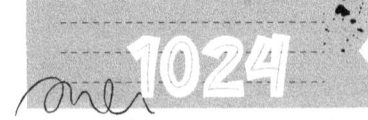

1024

In "Starlight" from Red, Taylor writes about an imaginary love story based on an old photo of Robert and Ethel Kennedy.

1025

The lyric "We're a crooked love in a straight line down" in "Treacherous" shows how a risky relationship can lead down a dangerous path.

1027

In Reputation, the song "So It Goes" uses the phrase "cut you like a knife" to show how sharp and painful relationships can be.

1026

In the Evermore album, the song "Gold Rush" talks about the envy and desire that comes with admiring someone who is highly desired by everyone.

1028

The golden glow in the "Daylight" music video shows how Taylor feels she has found real love and left behind the darker moments of her past.

1029

In Folklore, the song "Epiphany" is about finding peace in a chaotic world, with references to bravery and healing.

1031

The line "I was screaming long live all the magic we made" in Speak Now's "Long Live" is Taylor's way of thanking her fans for supporting her through her journey.

1030

The "Wonderland" music video from 1989 uses chess imagery, symbolizing the moves people make in relationships.

1032

In "You Are in Love" from 1989, the lyrics describe a perfect love story that Taylor witnessed between two of her close friends.

1033

In Red (Taylor's Version), the song "Message in a Bottle" is about sending a love message to someone far away, hoping they feel the same.

1034

The lyric "I polish up real nice" in "Bejeweled" from Midnights reflects how Taylor feels confident in her ability to shine, even after tough times.

1035

In "New Year's Day," the song's quiet piano and focus on the morning after a party shows how love continues even in ordinary moments.

Conclusion

Taylor Swift isn't just a superstar—she's a movement.

From her fearless beginnings to her chart-topping success, she's shown that being authentic, vulnerable, and true to yourself can make the impossible happen.

She's given us the songs that soundtrack our lives, from first crushes to heartaches to moments of pure joy.

And the best part?

She's done it all while staying connected to the people who matter most: her fans.

For years, Taylor has invited us into her world, and with every album, every surprise drop, every Easter egg, she's kept us on our toes, always wanting more.

Her evolution as an artist proves that change is not something to fear—it's something to embrace.

So what's next?

With Taylor, you never know, and that's what makes being a fan so exciting.

Whether it's a new sound, another surprise release, or even more hidden clues in her lyrics, one thing is for sure: she's always got something up her sleeve.

And as long as she's writing, performing, and connecting with us, we'll be there—ready for every twist, every anthem, and every story she has yet to tell.

Because with Taylor, it's not just music.

It's an adventure—and we're all in it together.

www.ingramcontent.com/pod-product-compliance
Lightning Source LLC
Chambersburg PA
CBHW070905120626
46546CB00001B/149